Disclosures

AI Disclosure, Fictional Work, Omissions, Not Instructional, and Full Liability Clause

This book was created with the assistance of artificial intelligence (AI). The content, including the storyline, characters, and events, is entirely fictional and intended for entertainment and educational purposes. Any resemblance to real persons, living or deceased, or real events is purely coincidental.

The use of AI technology in the creation of this work is meant to assist in the development and organization of ideas, enhance storytelling, and ensure a smooth flow of the narrative. All creative choices, plot developments, and character representations were made with the intention of supporting a fictional, imaginative narrative guided by the author's vision.

Omissions Clause

While every effort has been made to ensure the accuracy and completeness of the information provided in this work, some details may have been omitted, simplified, or altered to serve the fictional storyline. Any omissions or inconsistencies are unintentional and should not be interpreted as factual inaccuracies. The author and creators disclaim any liability for any errors, omissions, or interpretations that may arise from the content of this work.

Not Instructional Clause

This book is a work of fiction and is not intended to serve as an instructional guide or a reference for real-world actions, decisions, or situations. Any procedures, actions, or references to aviation, airports, aircraft, marine or other activities described in this book are purely for storytelling purposes and should not be followed, imitated, or applied to real-world situations. Readers should consult appropriate, qualified professionals for any instructional or technical guidance related to aviation or other fields mentioned in the book.

Full Liability Clause

The content in this book is provided on an "as is" basis and is purely for fictional entertainment. The author, creators, and any associated entities make no representations or warranties of any kind, express or implied, as to the accuracy, completeness, suitability, or reliability of the information, products, or services contained in this work for any purpose. The author and creators assume no responsibility for errors or omissions in the content, and no liability for any loss, damage, or harm of any kind incurred as a result of using, interpreting, or relying upon the content of this book.

By reading and engaging with this material, you acknowledge that the book is a work of fiction, and any actions taken based on the content are at your own risk. Under no circumstances shall the author, creators, or any related entities be held liable for any direct, indirect, incidental, special, or consequential damages arising from the use of this material, even if advised of the possibility of such damages.

Contents

Introduction

From the earliest days of human history, the dream of flight has captivated the imaginations of explorers, inventors, and dreamers alike. The desire to soar through the skies, to see the world from above, and to push the boundaries of what is possible has been a constant force driving technological innovation. But what if that dream didn't stop at the sky? What if we could not only fly, but also dive deep into the ocean, exploring the mysterious worlds beneath the surface with the same agility and freedom we experience in the air? This is the vision that inspired the creation of the Aqua-Flyer, a revolutionary aircraft capable of both aerial and underwater flight.

The Aqua-Flyer isn't just an aircraft—it represents a new era of exploration, one where the limitations of traditional aviation and underwater exploration are pushed aside in favor of seamless, amphibious travel. Combining the speed and maneuverability of an airplane with the depth capabilities of a submersible, the Aqua-Flyer allows scientists, military personnel, and explorers to transition effortlessly between air and water, unlocking new possibilities for research, rescue, and adventure.

For Jake, a young boy with a passion for flight, the Aqua-Flyer is more than just a machine—it's a gateway to his dreams. At just 10 years old, Jake has always been fascinated by airplanes and the thrill of exploration. When he's given the opportunity to be part of a mission aboard the Aqua-Flyer, he is thrust into a world far beyond anything he could have imagined. It's not just about flying—it's about learning, growing, and discovering how this extraordinary vehicle can reshape the future of exploration.

This story takes readers on an unforgettable journey through the eyes of Jake, as he navigates both the skies and the depths of the ocean aboard the Aqua-Flyer. Along the way, he learns about the incredible engineering feats that make amphibious flight possible, the teamwork required to operate such a complex machine, and the vast potential this technology holds for science, conservation, and even space exploration.

The Aqua-Flyer's development is a testament to human ingenuity and perseverance. Behind the scenes, dedicated teams of engineers, scientists, and technicians have worked tirelessly to bring this visionary concept to life. Their expertise in aerodynamics, propulsion systems, and marine research has allowed them to create a machine that not only defies conventional limitations but also opens up entirely new avenues for discovery. The lessons Jake learns from these experts go far beyond technical knowledge—they are lessons in focus, creativity, and dedication.

As you dive into this book, you'll not only follow Jake's thrilling adventure but also gain a deeper understanding of the real-world implications of amphibious flight. Whether it's the potential for environmental conservation, groundbreaking scientific research, or military operations that require rapid responses across different terrains, the Aqua-Flyer stands at the forefront of a new frontier. Its impact on future technologies, from ocean exploration to space travel, cannot be overstated.

The dream of flight has always been about more than just reaching new heights—it's about expanding our understanding of the world around us. The Aqua-Flyer, with its ability to bridge the gap between air and water, offers a glimpse into the future of exploration. As Jake embarks on his journey, we are reminded that the only limits to what we can achieve are the ones we place on ourselves. With focus, ingenuity, education, and commitment, the possibilities for discovery are truly endless.

Chapter 1: The Dream Begins

Jake had always been a dreamer, even as a little boy. While other kids spent their time running around or playing video games, Jake found himself staring at the sky, mesmerized by the sight of airplanes cutting through the clouds. There was something magical about the way those planes moved, gliding effortlessly, their engines roaring faintly in the distance. He couldn't help but imagine what it would be like to be up there, soaring above the world, free from the limits of the ground.

His love for planes started early. He could vividly recall his first visit to the local airfield with his dad. They had stood by the fence, watching planes take off and land. The noise, the smell of fuel, and the feeling of the ground trembling underfoot as a jet roared by had left a lasting impression on him. From that moment, Jake had been hooked. Airplanes weren't just machines to him—they were symbols of adventure, of breaking free, and of exploring the unknown.

Every day after school, Jake would rush home, drop his backpack at the door, and head straight to his room. His room was a testament to his passion. Posters of airplanes, from vintage warbirds to the most modern jets, covered the walls. His shelves were lined with model airplanes, each carefully assembled and painted to perfection. He spent hours reading books about aviation, from the Wright brothers' first flight to the most advanced aircraft of the modern era. His fascination with airplanes consumed him, and he loved every minute of it.

Jake's friends didn't quite share his enthusiasm. They were more interested in video games, sports, and other activities that didn't involve staring at the sky for hours. But that was okay with Jake. He didn't mind being different. In fact, he liked it. While they were content with their feet on the ground, Jake's mind was always soaring among the clouds. He didn't need anyone else to understand his dream, because it was his alone, and it was special.

One of Jake's favorite activities was building model airplanes. His father had bought him his first kit when he was seven, and ever since then, Jake had been hooked. There was something deeply satisfying about piecing together the tiny parts, carefully painting the fuselage, and attaching the wings. Once completed, he would proudly display each model on his shelves, often spending hours just admiring his handiwork. The models were more than just toys to Jake—they were tangible representations of his dream to one day fly for real.

His fascination with flight wasn't limited to models, though. Jake devoured every book and magazine he could find about airplanes and aviation. He knew the names of all the famous aircraft, from the Wright Flyer to the F-22 Raptor. He could recite facts about engine power, wingspans, and maximum speeds. His father often marveled at how much Jake seemed to know. For Jake, this wasn't just trivia—it was a connection to the world he longed to be part of.

Jake's father, while supportive, didn't share the same passion for flight. He was a marine biologist, more at home on the sea than in the air. Though they bonded over a love for exploration, Jake's dreams always pointed toward the sky, while his father's heart lay beneath the waves. Despite this, Jake's dad always encouraged his son's interests, making sure to fuel Jake's dreams in any way he could.

One evening, as Jake sat in his room, carefully adjusting the wings on his latest model, his father knocked on the door. Jake looked up, expecting the usual reminder about dinner or homework, but his dad had a different look on his face—one of excitement.

"Hey, Jake," his dad began, leaning against the doorframe. "You've been working hard on those models, huh?"

Jake nodded. "Yeah, this one's almost done. It's a replica of the SR-71 Blackbird."

His father chuckled. "Of course it is. Well, I've got something I think you might like. How would you feel about meeting someone who flies real planes for a living?"

Jake's eyes widened. "Are you serious?"

His dad smiled. "Absolutely. Remember my friend Mike? He's been a test pilot for years, and he's working on something pretty special right now. I thought it might be fun for you to meet him and see what he's up to."

Jake could hardly believe his ears. He knew about Mike Turner. His father had mentioned him a few times before, always with a sense of admiration. Mike was a test pilot for one of the most advanced aerospace companies in the world, flying planes that most people could only dream of. The idea of meeting him, of seeing the planes he flew, was almost too much for Jake to process.

"What's he working on?" Jake asked, his heart racing with excitement.

"Well," his dad said, stepping into the room and sitting on the edge of Jake's bed, "Mike and his team have been developing something pretty groundbreaking. It's not just any plane—it's a plane that can also travel underwater."

Jake blinked. "Underwater? Like a submarine?"

"Exactly," his dad replied, clearly enjoying Jake's reaction. "It's an amphibious aircraft, something that can take off from a runway, fly through the air, and then dive into the ocean like a submarine. It's still in the testing phase, but Mike thinks it's going to change the future of exploration."

Jake's mind raced with the possibilities. A plane that could also be a submarine? It sounded like something out of a science fiction movie, but here was his father telling him it was real. And he might actually get to see it.

"Can we go tomorrow?" Jake asked, barely able to contain his excitement.

His dad laughed. "I'll call Mike and see what we can arrange. But I think you're going to love it."

Jake spent the rest of the evening in a state of pure excitement. He could hardly concentrate on anything else as his mind buzzed with thoughts of what the next day might hold. Meeting Mike, seeing the amphibious plane—it was like all of his dreams were coming true at once. That night, as Jake lay in bed, he couldn't stop thinking about the possibilities. His imagination took him to the skies, flying above the clouds in an aircraft that could then dive beneath the ocean's surface, exploring the mysteries of the deep. It was a dream beyond anything he could have ever imagined.

The next morning, Jake was up before the sun, too excited to stay in bed. He dressed quickly and waited anxiously for his father to get ready. It felt like the longest wait of his life, but finally, they were in the car, heading to the aerospace facility where Mike worked.

As they drove, Jake's father explained more about Mike's project. The aircraft, called the Aqua-Flyer 1, was part of a new generation of amphibious vehicles that could revolutionize both aviation and marine exploration. The technology behind it was cutting-edge, allowing the craft to withstand the pressures of both high-altitude flight and deep-sea diving. It was, in every sense, a marvel of engineering.

When they arrived at the facility, Jake's excitement reached a new level. The building itself was interesting, with aircraft, massive hangars and runways stretching out in all directions. Security was tight, and Jake felt a thrill as they passed through the gates, knowing that he was about to see something truly extraordinary.

Mike greeted them at the entrance, a tall man with a broad smile and an air of confidence that only a test pilot could have. He wore a leather jacket and aviator sunglasses, looking every bit the part of the daring pilot Jake had imagined.

"Hey, Jake," Mike said, extending a hand. "I've heard a lot about you. Your dad tells me you're quite the aviation expert."

Jake shook his hand, grinning from ear to ear. "I love planes. I've been building models since I was seven."

Mike nodded, impressed. "Well, I think you're going to like what we've got inside. Follow me."

As they walked through the facility, Jake's eyes darted around, taking in every detail. Engineers and scientists were working on various projects, some of which looked like they belonged in the distant future rather than the present. But nothing could have prepared Jake for the sight that awaited him when they reached the hangar where the Aqua-Flyer 1 was housed.

The aircraft was unlike anything Jake had ever seen. Sleek and futuristic, it looked like a cross between a jet and a submarine, with smooth curves and powerful engines. It sat on the hangar floor, gleaming under the bright lights, ready for its next mission.

"This," Mike said, with a hint of pride in his voice, "is the Aqua-Flyer 1. She's still in the testing phase, but we're getting close. Once she's fully operational, she'll be able to take off from an airfield, soar through the skies, and then dive beneath the waves to explore the ocean depths."

Jake stared at the aircraft, speechless. It was even more incredible than he had imagined. The thought of flying in something like that, of experiencing both the air and the sea in the same machine, filled him with a sense of awe.

"Do you want to take a closer look?" Mike asked, noticing Jake's wide eyes.

Jake nodded eagerly, and they walked toward the aircraft. Up close, it was even more impressive. The technology involved in making something like this work was mind-boggling, and Jake couldn't wait to learn more about how it all came together.

For the next hour, Mike gave Jake and his dad a tour of the Aqua-Flyer, explaining the engineering behind it, the challenges of designing something that could handle both the skies and the deep ocean, and the potential it held for future exploration. Jake listened intently, absorbing every detail. This was more than just a plane—it was a glimpse into the future of aviation and exploration.

As the tour came to an end, Mike turned to Jake with a smile. "We've got a big test coming up soon, Jake. How would you feel about coming along for the ride? It could be a great opportunity for you to see how all of this works in action."

Jake's heart skipped a beat. Was he really being invited to join the test flight of the Aqua-Flyer? It was like something out of his wildest dreams.

"I'd love that!" Jake exclaimed, barely able to contain his excitement.

"Great," Mike said, clapping him on the shoulder. "We'll make it happen. You're in for one heck of an adventure, Jake."

As they left the facility and drove home, Jake couldn't stop smiling. His dream was about to take flight—literally. He was going to be part of something incredible, something that combined his love for airplanes with a whole new world of exploration. The sky was no longer the limit for Jake. The ocean, too, was waiting for him, and he couldn't wait to dive into the adventure.

That night, as he lay in bed, Jake's mind was filled with visions of soaring through the air and diving beneath the waves. The future had never looked so exciting. Tomorrow, the adventure would begin, and Jake knew that his life would never be the same again.

Chapter 2: The Amphibious Aircraft

Jake had hardly slept the night before. The anticipation of returning to the aerospace facility and seeing the Aqua-Flyer in action filled him with too much excitement to rest. Every time he closed his eyes, his mind played out scenarios where he was piloting the incredible craft, diving beneath the ocean's surface, and emerging from the depths like a bird of prey. It was beyond his wildest dreams, and now it was just within his grasp.

The next morning, Jake bounced out of bed and quickly got dressed. His dad, who had grown used to Jake's boundless energy when it came to anything related to planes, couldn't help but smile as he watched his son hurriedly shove down his breakfast.

"Slow down, Jake. We've got plenty of time," his dad said, though he understood his son's eagerness.

Jake grinned, his face flushed with excitement. "I know, Dad, but what if we get stuck in traffic or something? I don't want to be late."

His dad laughed softly and shook his head. "You've got nothing to worry about. Mike's probably just as excited to show you more of the Aqua-Flyer as you are to see it."

They set off in the car, the morning sun climbing higher into the sky as they drove toward the facility. As they approached the aerospace complex, Jake's heart pounded in his chest. The facility loomed ahead, a massive, high-tech complex filled with cutting-edge aircraft and the brightest minds in aviation engineering. It was a place Jake had only dreamed about before, but now it was becoming a key part of his life.

When they arrived, Mike was already waiting for them at the front entrance, leaning casually against a sleek electric vehicle. He greeted them with a wide grin, his aviator sunglasses reflecting the morning light. He looked every bit the daring pilot, and to Jake, Mike was quickly becoming a hero.

"Morning, Jake! Ready for another round?" Mike called out as they approached.

"More than ready!" Jake replied, practically bouncing on his toes.

"Good, because today's going to be pretty special. We're going to take a deeper dive—literally—into how the Aqua-Flyer works. I'm going to give you a hands-on tour, and if you're lucky, we might even take her for a spin," Mike said with a wink.

Jake's eyes widened at the prospect. "Seriously? I get to see it fly?"

"Maybe more than that," Mike said, his grin widening. "Come on, let's get started."

They walked through the sprawling complex, passing by hangars and labs where engineers worked on various projects. Jake's mind buzzed with questions, but he was too awestruck by everything around him to speak. The building buzzed with energy, like a hive of innovation and discovery, and Jake was in the center of it all.

As they approached the hangar where the Aqua-Flyer was stored, Mike began explaining more about the aircraft.

"The Aqua-Flyer is designed to do something no other craft can— seamlessly transition between air and water. It's been a dream of engineers for decades, but only recently have we had the technology to make it happen. The materials we use are both lightweight and incredibly strong, so it can handle the stresses of both high-altitude flight and deep-sea pressure."

Jake listened intently, soaking in every word. "How does it stay watertight when it goes underwater?"

"Good question," Mike said, clearly impressed by Jake's curiosity. "We use a combination of advanced composite materials and nanotechnology to create a seal that's completely watertight, even under extreme pressure. The aircraft's design also helps distribute the forces it encounters in the water, making it more stable than anything else out there."

Jake was amazed. "That's incredible."

"Yeah, it is," Mike agreed. "But what's even more amazing is what it can do once it's underwater. Most submarines are pretty slow and clunky, but the Aqua-Flyer? She can move like a fish. We've designed the wings to fold back and act like fins, and the thrusters can rotate to give us incredible maneuverability."

As Mike talked, they reached the hangar doors. With a swipe of his keycard, the massive doors slid open, revealing the Aqua-Flyer in all its futuristic glory. Bathed in the glow of the hangar lights, it looked even more magnificent than Jake remembered. Its sleek, silver body gleamed under the lights, and the sharp angles of its wings made it look like it was in motion, even though it was standing still.

"Wow," Jake whispered, his eyes wide as he took in the sight of the aircraft.

Mike led them closer, and as they approached the Aqua-Flyer, Jake could see the details up close. The craft was bigger than it had looked from afar, with its powerful engines and complex array of control surfaces.

"You're looking at the future of exploration," Mike said proudly. "Not just for aviation, but for the oceans as well. This baby can go anywhere—high up in the stratosphere or deep down in the trenches of the sea."

Jake couldn't help but reach out and touch the cold metal surface of the aircraft, feeling the cool, smooth texture beneath his fingertips. It felt almost otherworldly, like something out of science fiction.

"Want to see inside?" Mike asked, noticing Jake's awe-struck expression.

Jake nodded enthusiastically, and Mike led them to the side of the craft, where a small hatch opened with a soft hiss. Inside was the cockpit, a cramped but highly advanced control center filled with touchscreens, buttons, and switches. The seat looked like something from a spaceship, designed to keep the pilot safe and comfortable during both flight and underwater travel.

"This is where the magic happens," Mike said, gesturing to the cockpit. "Everything in here is state-of-the-art. We've got advanced navigation systems, real-time data feeds from the ocean and the atmosphere, and controls that can switch between flight mode and submarine mode in seconds."

Jake stepped inside the cockpit, his heart pounding. The seat felt comfortable as he sat down, and he ran his hands over the controls. He imagined himself flying the Aqua-Flyer, taking off into the sky before diving into the ocean. The thought sent a thrill through him.

"How does it work underwater?" Jake asked, looking up at Mike.

"Once we're in the water, the plane essentially becomes a submarine. The engines switch to a different mode that uses the water for propulsion, and the wings retract to reduce drag. It's fast, too—faster than most submarines out there."

Jake marveled at the technology. He had read about submarines before, but none of them were anything like this. The idea of combining the freedom of flight with the ability to explore the ocean was almost too incredible to believe.

Mike pointed to the control panel. "Want to try running through a few of the simulations? It's like a video game, but a little more complicated."

Jake's eyes lit up. "Can I?"

"Of course," Mike said, reaching over to activate the simulator. "This will give you a feel for how the Aqua-Flyer handles in the air and underwater. It's a bit tricky at first, but I think you'll pick it up pretty quickly."

Jake gripped the controls as the screen in front of him lit up with a simulation of the aircraft taking off. The simulation was so realistic that it felt like he was really in the air, flying above the clouds. The controls were responsive, and as Jake tilted the joystick, the Aqua-Flyer moved smoothly through the sky.

"This is amazing!" Jake exclaimed as he guided the aircraft through the simulation.

Mike chuckled. "You're a natural. Now let's switch to submarine mode."

With a flick of a switch, the simulation shifted. The plane dove down, transitioning smoothly from the sky into the ocean. The controls changed, too, as Jake navigated the Aqua-Flyer through the water, dodging coral reefs and schools of fish.

Jake could hardly believe how different the craft felt underwater. The resistance of the water made the controls heavier, but the Aqua-Flyer moved gracefully, like a fish swimming through the sea. It was a whole new world, and Jake was completely immersed in it.

As the simulation ended, Jake sat back in the seat, his heart racing with excitement. He had never experienced anything like that before. It was as if he had truly been flying and diving beneath the waves.

"That was incredible," Jake said, still breathless from the excitement.

Mike smiled. "Glad you enjoyed it. You've got a real knack for this, Jake. Who knows—maybe one day you'll be flying one of these for real."

Jake grinned, the idea thrilling him to his core. Flying the Aqua-Flyer in a real mission was beyond anything he had ever imagined, but now, it didn't seem so far-fetched.

"Do you think I'll get to see it fly for real?" Jake asked, his voice full of hope.

"Well, that's the plan," Mike said. "We've got a test flight scheduled for tomorrow. If everything goes well, you might just get to see it in action— and maybe even take a short ride."

Jake's heart leaped at the prospect. Tomorrow couldn't come fast enough.

Chapter 3: Into the Abyss

The day Jake had been waiting for finally arrived. He barely slept the night before, his mind racing with anticipation of what the Aqua-Flyer's first mission would bring. Today, he wouldn't just be watching from the sidelines; he'd be a part of the crew. The thought filled him with both excitement and nervousness. As he got dressed that morning, he couldn't help but wonder what kinds of challenges awaited them beneath the ocean's surface.

At breakfast, Jake's dad noticed the excitement written all over his face. "Ready for the big day?" his dad asked, passing him a plate of toast.

Jake nodded eagerly, unable to contain the grin spreading across his face. "I've been ready since yesterday."

His dad chuckled, giving him an encouraging pat on the back. "It's going to be an incredible experience, Jake. Just remember to pay attention to everything Captain Mike and the crew teach you. It's not all fun and games—this is serious stuff."

"I know, Dad," Jake said. "I'll be careful."

They arrived at the aerospace facility just as the sun was rising. The sky was painted in hues of orange and pink, and Jake could feel the crisp morning air buzzing with energy. Today wasn't just any day—it was the beginning of something extraordinary.

As they approached the hangar where the Aqua-Flyer was housed, Jake saw Captain Mike standing outside, talking with the other scientists and engineers. His presence alone was enough to calm Jake's nerves. Mike had a way of making everything seem like an adventure, even the most technical details of the mission.

"Morning, Jake!" Mike greeted him with a broad smile, walking over to meet them. "You ready for the big flight?"

Jake nodded, trying to appear more confident than he felt. "I think so."

Mike gave him a friendly clap on the shoulder. "Don't worry. You'll do great. Just stick close to me, and I'll show you the ropes."

They entered the hangar, and there she was—the Aqua-Flyer, gleaming under the bright lights like a bird poised to take flight. It was even more magnificent today, knowing that it was about to embark on its maiden voyage into the deep sea. Jake's heart swelled with excitement.

The team went over the final checks, ensuring that every system on the Aqua-Flyer was functioning perfectly. The engineers hovered around the aircraft, running diagnostics on the engines, the flight control system, and the underwater thrusters. Jake watched in awe as they worked, their hands moving with practiced precision over the complex controls and equipment.

Mike turned to Jake, sensing his curiosity. "Want to know what all this is for?"

Jake nodded. "Yeah, what are they doing?"

"They're running the pre-flight checks," Mike explained. "Before we take off, we need to make sure every part of the Aqua-Flyer is in perfect working order. If even one system isn't functioning properly, it could cause problems once we're in the air—or worse, underwater."

Jake's stomach fluttered at the mention of problems. "What kind of problems?"

"Well," Mike said, scratching his chin thoughtfully, "if the pressure systems aren't calibrated correctly, we could have issues when we dive. The deeper we go, the more pressure the Aqua-Flyer will face, and if something's off, it could compromise the hull."

Jake's eyes widened. "But everything's going to be fine, right?"

Mike gave him a reassuring smile. "Don't worry. That's why we run these checks. By the time we're ready to take off, we'll know everything is perfect."

Jake nodded, though a small knot of anxiety remained in his stomach. He knew this mission wasn't without risks, but he trusted Mike and the team. They were professionals, and they had done this sort of thing before—just not with a craft that could fly and dive into the depths of the ocean.

Once the checks were complete, it was time to board. Jake followed Mike up the ladder to the cockpit, his heart pounding in his chest. He couldn't believe this was actually happening. He was going to be on a real mission with a real crew, flying in the most advanced aircraft ever built.

Inside the cockpit, everything was sleek and futuristic. The control panels glowed with soft light, and the seat Jake settled into felt like it was designed for comfort and safety. Mike sat beside him in the pilot's seat, adjusting the controls and checking the instruments.

"All set, Jake?" Mike asked, glancing over at him.

Jake nodded, swallowing hard. "Yeah. I'm ready."

"Good. This is going to be fun."

With a flick of a few switches, the Aqua-Flyer's engines roared to life. The sound reverberated through the cockpit, making Jake's heart race even faster. It felt like pure power, like nothing he'd ever experienced before. As the aircraft taxied out of the hangar and onto the runway, Jake's excitement reached a fever pitch.

The Aqua-Flyer picked up speed, and before Jake could even process what was happening, they were airborne. The ground fell away beneath them, and the sky stretched out endlessly in all directions. Jake pressed his face to the window, watching in awe as the landscape shrank beneath them, the clouds enveloping the craft as they climbed higher and higher.

"This is amazing!" Jake exclaimed, unable to contain his excitement.

Mike chuckled. "And we haven't even gotten to the best part yet."

They flew over the ocean, the vast expanse of water shimmering beneath them like a giant, glistening mirror. The Aqua-Flyer's engines hummed steadily, and the craft sliced through the air with the precision of a hawk on the hunt.

"Alright, Jake," Mike said after a while, his tone growing more serious. "We're about to begin the descent into the water. This is where things get interesting."

Jake's heart skipped a beat. The descent into the water. He had read about it, dreamed about it, but now it was actually happening. He tightened his grip on the armrests, his mind racing with anticipation.

Mike adjusted the controls, and Jake felt the Aqua-Flyer start to descend. The ocean rushed up toward them, and before he knew it, they were skimming just above the surface of the water. The transition was so smooth that Jake barely felt it when they made contact with the waves.

The Aqua-Flyer plunged beneath the surface, and Jake's world transformed. The light from the sun filtered through the water, casting an eerie, blue glow throughout the cockpit. Schools of fish darted past the windows, and the deeper they went, the more surreal the environment became. It was like entering another world—one that was both beautiful and terrifying.

"We're officially underwater," Mike said, his voice calm and steady. "Welcome to the abyss."

Jake could hardly believe his eyes. The ocean around them was vast and endless, filled with creatures he had only ever seen in documentaries. As they descended deeper, the light from the surface grew dimmer, replaced by the eerie glow of bioluminescent creatures that flickered like stars in the darkness.

"This is incredible," Jake whispered, his breath fogging the window as he leaned closer.

Mike nodded, his eyes focused on the controls. "And we're just getting started. The deeper we go, the more amazing things we'll see."

They descended further, the pressure outside the craft increasing with every meter. The Aqua-Flyer's systems adjusted automatically, ensuring that they remained safe and comfortable inside. Jake marveled at the technology that made this possible. Just days ago, the thought of flying an aircraft that could dive into the ocean had seemed impossible. Now, he was living it.

Suddenly, a large shadow loomed in the distance. Jake squinted, trying to make out what it was. As they got closer, the shape became clearer—a massive school of manta rays gliding gracefully through the water.

"Whoa," Jake breathed. "Look at that!"

Mike smiled. "Impressive, isn't it? These creatures are perfectly adapted to life in the ocean. They move with such grace, like they're flying underwater."

Jake watched in awe as the manta rays swam past, their enormous wings flapping gently as they glided through the water. It was a sight he would never forget.

As they continued their descent, the landscape below them changed. The seafloor came into view, a rugged terrain of mountains and valleys, dotted with strange formations Jake had never seen before. Some of the rocks glowed faintly, emitting a soft, otherworldly light.

"That's part of the hydrothermal vent system," Mike explained, pointing to the glowing rocks. "These vents release hot water and minerals from deep within the Earth's crust. They create entire ecosystems down here, supporting life where we once thought none could exist."

Jake's eyes widened. "So there are creatures living down there?"

"Absolutely," Mike said. "Some of the most unique and bizarre life forms on the planet live around these vents. You'll see."

Jake's curiosity was piqued. The thought of discovering new life forms deep beneath the ocean's surface filled him with excitement. He leaned forward in his seat, eager to see what lay ahead.

As they approached the hydrothermal vents, the water around them became warmer. Strange creatures began to appear—giant tube worms, crabs with long, spindly legs, and fish with glowing eyes that seemed to peer right into Jake's soul.

"This is incredible," Jake said, his voice barely above a whisper. "How do these things survive down here?"

Mike smiled. "It's all about adaptation. These creatures have evolved to thrive in conditions that would kill most other animals. The heat from the vents provides the energy they need, and the minerals in the water give them the nutrients to survive. It's a completely different world down here."

Jake was mesmerized. He had always been fascinated by airplanes, but this—this was something entirely new. The ocean was a world of its own, full of wonders he had never even imagined.

They hovered near the vents for a while, observing the life forms that called this harsh environment home. Jake could see the scientists in the back of the Aqua-Flyer taking notes and collecting data, their expressions filled with awe and excitement.

Just as Jake was starting to feel comfortable in this strange new world, something unexpected happened. The Aqua-Flyer shuddered, and a loud beeping sound filled the cockpit.

Mike's hands flew to the controls, his expression serious. "Hang on, Jake. We've got a situation."

"What's happening?" Jake asked, his heart pounding in his chest.

"We've hit an underwater current," Mike explained, his voice calm but focused. "It's stronger than we anticipated. I'm going to have to make some adjustments to keep us stable."

Jake's stomach lurched as the Aqua-Flyer was pushed to the side, the current threatening to drag them off course. Mike worked quickly, adjusting the thrusters and stabilizers to counteract the force of the water. The beeping continued, but after a tense few moments, the Aqua-Flyer leveled out, and the beeping stopped.

Jake let out a breath he hadn't realized he'd been holding. "That was intense."

Mike gave him a reassuring smile. "It's all part of the job. The ocean is unpredictable, but we're equipped to handle it. Just keep your eyes open and stay alert."

Jake nodded, his heart still racing. He had always known that exploration came with risks, but experiencing it firsthand was a different story. Despite the scare, he was more determined than ever to see this mission through.

Chapter 4: The Depths of Discovery

The Aqua-Flyer continued its descent into the deep, dark waters, where sunlight could no longer penetrate. Jake peered out of the window, his face pressed against the cold glass. It felt as if they were venturing into another world, one that was as mysterious and alien as any far-off planet. The bioluminescent glow of creatures illuminated the inky blackness outside, flickering like stars in a sea of darkness. It was both mesmerizing and eerie.

Mike had been quiet for a few minutes, focused on navigating the Aqua-Flyer through the increasingly difficult conditions. The water pressure was mounting with every meter they descended, and the strain on the craft was noticeable. Jake could hear the faint groaning of the hull as it adjusted to the pressure. The Aqua-Flyer was designed for these depths, but even with its advanced engineering, Jake could feel the weight of the ocean pressing in on them.

"Everything okay?" Jake asked, glancing over at Mike.

Mike nodded, though his expression was tense. "We're pushing the limits of what this craft can handle, but she's holding up well. The deeper we go, the more pressure we face. The Aqua-Flyer's designed for this, but we still have to be careful. It's uncharted territory down here."

Jake's heart skipped a beat at the words "uncharted territory." It was both thrilling and terrifying. He couldn't help but wonder what else lurked in these depths. His imagination ran wild with thoughts of giant sea creatures, shipwrecks, and unexplored caverns. The idea that they were some of the first humans to ever reach these depths filled him with a sense of awe.

Outside, the landscape was changing. The seafloor was no longer just a barren expanse of sand and rock. Strange, tall structures began to appear, like chimneys spewing smoke. At first, Jake thought it was volcanic activity, but as they got closer, he realized they were something entirely different.

"Those are the hydrothermal vents I told you about," Mike said, noticing Jake's wide-eyed expression. "They release superheated water and minerals from the Earth's crust. These vents create unique ecosystems that are home to some of the most unusual creatures on the planet."

Jake leaned closer to the window, fascinated by the towering structures. The vents glowed faintly, casting an eerie light on the surrounding seafloor. Around them, creatures moved—giant tube worms that swayed gently in the current, crabs with spindly legs scuttling across the rocks, and fish with glowing eyes that seemed to appear out of nowhere.

"This is incredible," Jake whispered, his breath fogging the glass as he spoke. "I've never seen anything like it."

Mike smiled, though his eyes remained fixed on the controls. "Not many people have. The deep sea is one of the least explored places on Earth. We know more about the surface of the moon than we do about what's down here."

Jake couldn't wrap his head around that. It seemed impossible that in an age of satellites and space exploration, so much of the ocean remained a mystery. But as he stared out into the dark, vast expanse, he understood. The ocean was a world unto itself, and it was only now, with technology like the Aqua-Flyer, that humanity was beginning to uncover its secrets.

Suddenly, the Aqua-Flyer's control panel beeped, and a flashing red light appeared on one of the monitors. Jake's stomach tightened. He recognized that sound—it was the same alarm that had gone off when they hit the underwater current.

Mike frowned, quickly analyzing the data on the screen. "We're hitting stronger pressure down here than anticipated. The vents are releasing a lot of energy, and it's creating turbulence in the water."

Jake glanced nervously at the hull. He could hear the groaning of the metal growing louder, and the Aqua-Flyer shuddered as the turbulence hit them. The craft rocked slightly from side to side, and Jake gripped the armrests of his seat to steady himself.

"Is it safe?" Jake asked, his voice betraying a hint of fear.

Mike didn't answer right away, his focus entirely on the controls. After a few tense moments, he spoke. "We're fine, but I'm going to keep us at this depth for a while. We can't push the Aqua-Flyer any further without risking damage. The pressure is too intense down here."

Jake nodded, though his heart was still racing. The excitement of the adventure was tinged with the reality of the dangers they faced. This wasn't just a joyride—this was real exploration, with real risks. But even with the fear gnawing at his gut, Jake couldn't deny the thrill of being part of something so groundbreaking.

They hovered near the hydrothermal vents, the Aqua-Flyer's systems stabilizing as Mike expertly navigated them through the turbulence.

Jake watched in awe as more creatures emerged from the darkness, drawn to the heat and energy of the vents. It was like watching a scene from a documentary, but this was real, happening right in front of him.

"Look at that," Jake said, pointing to a massive crab that was scuttling across the rocks near the vent. Its legs were long and spindly, and its shell was covered in strange, barnacle-like growths. "What kind of crab is that?"

Mike glanced at it, then smiled. "That's a Yeti crab. They live down here near the vents, feeding off the bacteria that thrive in these extreme conditions. They've got hairy arms, which is how they got their name."

Jake stared in amazement. "That's wild."

"It's just one of many strange creatures that live down here," Mike said. "The deep sea is full of surprises. There's a whole world down here that we're only beginning to understand."

As they continued to observe the vents, the scientists on board the Aqua-Flyer began their work. They used robotic arms to collect samples of the water and minerals around the vents, as well as data on the creatures that lived there. Jake watched them work, fascinated by the precision and care they took with every task. It was clear that this mission wasn't just about exploration—it was about discovery, about pushing the boundaries of human knowledge.

Jake felt a sense of pride swell in his chest. He was part of something important, something that could change the way people thought about the ocean and the creatures that lived in its depths. For the first time, he understood why his dad had dedicated his life to studying marine biology. There was so much to learn, so much to discover, and being on the cutting edge of that knowledge was an incredible feeling.

As the hours passed, Jake continued to take in the sights around them. The deeper they went, the stranger and more alien the creatures became. At one point, they passed a jellyfish that was unlike anything Jake had ever seen. Its body was almost completely transparent, and it emitted a soft, pulsing glow that lit up the water around it. Its long, trailing tentacles swayed gently in the current, giving it an ethereal, ghost-like appearance.

"That's a Deepstaria jellyfish," Mike explained, noticing Jake's awe. "They're pretty rare. They live in the deep sea and have these huge, umbrella-like bodies that can expand and contract to catch prey."

Jake couldn't tear his eyes away from the jellyfish as it drifted past them, its glowing body casting a soft light on the Aqua-Flyer's hull. It was beautiful in a strange, otherworldly way, and Jake felt a shiver run down his spine as he watched it disappear into the darkness.

"There's so much we don't know about the deep sea," Mike said quietly. "Every time we come down here, we discover something new. It's like exploring an alien planet, right here on Earth."

Jake nodded, understanding exactly what he meant. The ocean was vast and full of mystery, and they were only scratching the surface of what it had to offer.

Just as Jake was starting to feel comfortable in this strange new world, the Aqua-Flyer's alarms went off again. This time, the sound was sharper, more urgent. The control panel lit up with a flurry of red lights, and Mike's expression turned serious.

"What's happening?" Jake asked, his heart pounding.

Mike's hands moved quickly over the controls. "We've got a pressure issue. The deeper we go, the more stress the hull is under. I'm going to have to bring us up a little. We're pushing the limits down here."

Jake swallowed hard, feeling the weight of the ocean pressing down on them. The Aqua-Flyer shuddered again, and Jake could hear the groaning of the hull growing louder. Mike's fingers flew over the controls as he adjusted the craft's altitude, slowly bringing them back up to a safer depth.

The tension in the cockpit was palpable. Even the scientists in the back had stopped their work, their eyes fixed on the monitors. Jake's heart raced as he watched Mike work, trusting him to keep them safe. After what felt like an eternity, the alarms stopped, and the Aqua-Flyer leveled out.

Mike let out a breath and leaned back in his seat, his shoulders relaxing. "That was close. We're fine now, but we'll need to be careful how deep we go from here."

Jake nodded, though his hands were still shaking. He hadn't realized just how dangerous this mission could be. The ocean was a force to be reckoned with, and despite the Aqua-Flyer's advanced technology, there were limits to what they could do down here.

As they continued to hover near the hydrothermal vents, the team resumed their work. Jake watched as the robotic arms collected more samples and the scientists monitored the data. The sense of urgency from earlier had passed, but the tension remained. They were in uncharted waters, both literally and figuratively, and there was no telling what challenges lay ahead.

Suddenly, one of the scientists let out a gasp, drawing everyone's attention. "Look at this!" she exclaimed, pointing to one of the monitors.

Jake leaned over to see what she was looking at. The screen displayed an image of a creature that Jake had never seen before. It looked like a cross between a squid and a jellyfish, with long, flowing tentacles and a translucent body. Its eyes glowed faintly in the darkness, and it moved with a grace that was almost hypnotic.

"What is that?" Jake asked, his voice filled with wonder.

The scientist shook her head, her eyes wide with excitement. "I don't know. I've never seen anything like it."

Mike glanced at the screen, his expression thoughtful. "We might have just discovered a new species."

The excitement in the cockpit was electric. Everyone was leaning forward, watching the creature as it floated past the Aqua-Flyer. Jake's heart raced with the thrill of discovery. This was what exploration was all about—finding the unknown, pushing the boundaries of what was possible, and uncovering the secrets of the world around them.

As the creature disappeared into the darkness, the team quickly began analyzing the data they had collected. Jake watched as the scientists worked, their faces lit up with excitement and determination. They were on the verge of something big, and Jake felt honored to be a part of it.

"We're going to have to return to the surface soon," Mike said after a while, glancing at the time. "We've collected a lot of valuable data, and it's time to head back. But don't worry, Jake—we'll be back down here soon enough."

Jake nodded, though he was reluctant to leave. The deep sea had captured his imagination in a way he hadn't expected. He had always dreamed of flying, of soaring through the skies, but now he realized that the ocean held just as many wonders as the air. There was so much left to discover, and Jake couldn't wait to see what the future held.

As the Aqua-Flyer began its ascent, Jake stared out of the window, watching the strange and wonderful creatures fade into the distance.

The ocean was vast, mysterious, and full of surprises, and Jake knew that this was only the beginning of his journey.

Chapter 5: Underwater Flight

As the Aqua-Flyer ascended from the depths, Jake's mind raced with everything he had just experienced. The wonders of the deep sea, the strange creatures, the hydrothermal vents—it was almost too much to take in. He felt like he had been part of something truly extraordinary, and yet he knew that this was only the beginning of his adventure.

The Aqua-Flyer emerged from the darkness, breaking through the layer where sunlight began to filter through the water. The transition from the shadowy abyss to the lighter waters felt surreal. Jake pressed his face against the window, watching as schools of brightly colored fish darted by, their scales shimmering in the dappled sunlight.

Mike adjusted the controls, guiding the Aqua-Flyer smoothly through the water. The craft moved with a grace that Jake hadn't expected, gliding effortlessly through the ocean like a giant sea creature itself. He marveled at how different the experience of flying underwater was compared to flying in the air.

"You doing okay over there?" Mike asked, glancing over at Jake.

Jake nodded, still awestruck by everything he was seeing. "Yeah, this is amazing."

Mike smiled. "Glad to hear it. You've been handling everything like a pro so far. How about we take it up a notch?"

Jake's heart skipped a beat. "What do you mean?"

"I mean," Mike said, his grin widening, "how would you like to take the controls for a bit?"

Jake blinked in surprise. "You mean...fly the Aqua-Flyer? For real?"

"For real," Mike confirmed. "We're in a pretty safe area right now, and I think you're ready to give it a shot. I'll be right here with you, of course, but I think it's time you got a feel for how this baby handles underwater."

Jake couldn't believe what he was hearing. The thought of actually controlling the Aqua-Flyer, even for a few minutes, sent a thrill of excitement through him. He had always dreamed of flying a plane, but this—flying a plane that could also move underwater—was beyond anything he could have imagined.

"Are you serious?" Jake asked, his voice barely above a whisper.

Mike chuckled. "I wouldn't joke about something like this. You up for it?"

Jake's nerves buzzed with both excitement and anxiety. What if he messed up? What if he accidentally crashed the Aqua-Flyer into something? But as he looked at Mike, who was watching him with calm confidence, Jake felt a surge of determination. This was a once-in-a-lifetime opportunity, and he wasn't about to pass it up.

"I'm ready," Jake said, his voice filled with resolve.

"Alright, then," Mike said, his fingers flying over the controls as he switched the Aqua-Flyer into manual mode. "I'm going to show you the basics first, and then it's all yours."

Jake nodded, trying to focus as Mike explained how the Aqua-Flyer's controls worked underwater. The craft's thrusters could rotate in different directions, allowing it to move up, down, forward, and sideways with ease. The wings, which had retracted when they entered the water, acted like fins, helping to steer the craft through the currents. It was similar to flying in the air, but with much more resistance from the water.

"The key is to think of it like swimming," Mike said, adjusting the thrusters as he demonstrated. "The water creates a lot of drag, so your movements need to be smooth and controlled. Don't try to jerk the controls like you would in the air. It's all about finesse down here."

Jake watched intently, trying to absorb everything Mike was telling him. He could feel the difference in how the Aqua-Flyer moved compared to when it was in the air. Every adjustment took a little more effort, and the water pushed back against the craft, making it feel heavier.

"Okay," Mike said after a few minutes. "Your turn."

Jake's hands trembled slightly as he reached for the controls. He took a deep breath, trying to steady himself. This was it—the moment he had been dreaming of for as long as he could remember. With Mike's guidance, he placed his hands on the joystick and throttle, feeling the smooth, cool metal beneath his fingers.

"Take it slow," Mike said, his voice calm and steady. "Just ease the throttle forward a bit and see how she responds."

Jake nodded, his heart pounding in his chest. He gently pushed the throttle forward, and the Aqua-Flyer responded immediately, gliding forward through the water with a smooth, graceful motion. It was like riding a wave, the craft cutting through the water with ease. Jake could feel the resistance of the water, but it wasn't overwhelming. It was like swimming, just as Mike had said.

"That's it," Mike said encouragingly. "Nice and easy. You're doing great."

Jake's confidence grew as he guided the Aqua-Flyer through the water. The controls felt natural in his hands, and he began to get a feel for how the craft moved. He adjusted the thrusters slightly, steering the Aqua-Flyer to the left, then to the right. Each movement was smooth and controlled, just as Mike had instructed.

"This is incredible," Jake said, his voice filled with wonder. "It feels like I'm flying underwater."

"That's exactly what you're doing," Mike said with a grin. "You're flying in one of the most challenging environments on Earth. And you're doing it like a pro."

Jake beamed with pride. He had always dreamed of flying, but he never imagined it would feel like this. The combination of the water's resistance and the craft's power made for a unique experience, one that Jake knew he would never forget.

"Want to try going a little deeper?" Mike asked.

Jake hesitated for a moment, but the excitement quickly outweighed his nerves. "Yeah, let's do it."

"Alright," Mike said, adjusting the controls slightly to give Jake more control over the descent. "Take it slow and keep an eye on the depth gauge. We don't want to go too deep, but I think you're ready to explore a little more."

Jake nodded, his hands steady on the controls. He gently eased the thrusters downward, and the Aqua-Flyer began to descend. The water grew darker as they went deeper, and Jake could feel the pressure increasing. It wasn't as intense as when they had been near the hydrothermal vents, but it was enough to remind him of the power of the ocean.

As they descended, new creatures began to appear outside the windows. Jake spotted a group of jellyfish, their translucent bodies glowing faintly in the dim light. Their long, trailing tentacles swayed gently in the water, creating an almost hypnotic effect.

"Those are Moon Jellyfish," Mike said, pointing them out. "They're harmless, but they're beautiful, aren't they?"

Jake nodded, mesmerized by the sight. The jellyfish floated past the Aqua-Flyer, their glowing bodies casting a soft light on the hull. It was like watching a ballet, the jellyfish moving with a grace that seemed almost otherworldly.

"You're doing great, Jake," Mike said, his voice filled with pride. "Keep it up."

Jake's confidence continued to grow as he guided the Aqua-Flyer deeper into the ocean. He adjusted the thrusters, steering the craft around a large coral formation that rose up from the seafloor like a giant, living mountain. The coral was teeming with life—colorful fish darted in and out of the crevices, while strange, spiny creatures clung to the rocks.

"That's a coral reef," Mike explained. "They're like underwater cities, home to thousands of species of marine life. It's one of the most important ecosystems in the ocean."

Jake marveled at the sight. The reef was alive with color and movement, a bustling metropolis beneath the waves. He could see schools of fish swimming in perfect synchronization, their scales shimmering in the dim light. It was a sight he had only ever seen in documentaries, and now he was witnessing it firsthand.

As they continued to explore, Jake grew more comfortable with the controls. He experimented with different movements, guiding the Aqua-Flyer in slow, sweeping arcs through the water. The craft responded beautifully, gliding through the ocean with a grace that made Jake feel like he was part of the water itself.

"How does it feel?" Mike asked, watching Jake with a smile.

"It feels amazing," Jake said, his voice filled with excitement. "It's like nothing I've ever done before. It's so different from flying in the air."

"That's because the water creates so much more resistance than air," Mike explained. "But once you get used to it, it's just as exhilarating. You're doing a great job, Jake."

Jake beamed with pride. He couldn't believe how natural it felt to control the Aqua-Flyer. It was as if all the hours he had spent dreaming about flying were finally paying off. And now, here he was, flying not just through the air, but through the ocean itself.

Suddenly, something caught Jake's eye. In the distance, a large shadow was moving toward them. At first, Jake thought it was a school of fish, but as it got closer, he realized it was something much bigger.

"Mike," Jake said, his voice filled with a mixture of excitement and nervousness. "What's that?"

Mike squinted at the shadow, then his eyes widened. "That's a whale."

Jake's heart skipped a beat. A whale? He had never seen one in real life before, and the thought of being so close to such a massive creature sent a thrill through him.

The whale came closer, and Jake could see its enormous body moving gracefully through the water. It was a blue whale, the largest animal on the planet, and it dwarfed the Aqua-Flyer. Its massive tail fin moved slowly, propelling it forward with effortless power.

"That's a blue whale," Mike said, his voice filled with awe. "They're the biggest animals on Earth. They can grow up to a hundred feet long."

Jake stared in amazement as the whale swam past them. It was so big that it made the Aqua-Flyer feel like a toy in comparison. The whale's skin was covered in scars and barnacles, evidence of its long life in the ocean. Despite its size, it moved with a grace that was almost hypnotic.

"Wow," Jake whispered, his eyes wide with wonder. "It's huge."

Mike nodded. "They're gentle giants. They feed on tiny creatures called krill, which they filter through their baleen plates. They're some of the most magnificent creatures in the ocean."

Jake watched as the whale continued on its way, its massive tail fin disappearing into the distance. He felt a sense of awe wash over him. The ocean was full of incredible creatures, and he had only just begun to scratch the surface of what it had to offer.

"That was amazing," Jake said, still in awe of what he had just seen.

Mike smiled. "You did great, Jake. You handled the Aqua-Flyer like a pro, and you got to see one of the most incredible animals on the planet. Not bad for your first time flying underwater, huh?"

Jake grinned, his heart swelling with pride. "Yeah, not bad at all."

As the Aqua-Flyer continued to glide through the water, Jake felt a sense of peace wash over him. He had always dreamed of flying, but now he realized that the ocean held just as much wonder and excitement as the skies. There was so much left to explore, so much left to discover, and Jake couldn't wait to see what the future held.

Chapter 6: Deep-Sea Dangers

The exhilaration of piloting the Aqua-Flyer still hadn't worn off as Jake leaned back in his seat, grinning from ear to ear. The feeling of flying underwater, navigating through the vast ocean, and encountering creatures as magnificent as the blue whale was beyond anything he could have imagined. But as the Aqua-Flyer continued its journey through the deep, a new tension began to fill the cockpit.

Mike's expression had shifted, his usual calm demeanor replaced with a look of concentration. Jake noticed the faint hum of the Aqua-Flyer's engines had changed, becoming lower and more strained. The soft vibration of the controls beneath Jake's hands felt different now, more pronounced, as if the craft was fighting against the water.

"Everything okay?" Jake asked, trying to keep his voice steady.

Mike glanced at the control panel, his fingers moving quickly over the buttons and switches. "We're hitting some trouble. The pressure down here is getting stronger, and the Aqua-Flyer's systems are starting to strain. We might have a mechanical issue."

Jake's heart skipped a beat. Mechanical issue? The words echoed in his mind, bringing with them a wave of uncertainty. He had known from the start that exploring the deep ocean wasn't without its dangers, but hearing it confirmed from Mike sent a shiver down his spine.

"What kind of issue?" Jake asked, his voice quieter now.

Mike's eyes stayed fixed on the panel as he adjusted the thrusters. "It looks like one of the stabilizers is malfunctioning. The pressure is throwing off the system that keeps us balanced. We're going to need to act fast before it gets worse."

Jake swallowed hard, gripping the armrests of his seat. The Aqua-Flyer shuddered again, and the groaning sound of the hull was growing louder. Outside the window, the water seemed darker, heavier, as if the ocean itself was pressing in on them.

"Is there anything I can do to help?" Jake asked, his nerves buzzing with a mixture of fear and determination.

Mike glanced at him, his face serious but calm. "I might need you to monitor the pressure readings while I work on stabilizing the craft. If the pressure increases too much, we'll have to ascend quickly."

Jake nodded, his heart pounding. This wasn't a game anymore. The mission had suddenly become very real, and very dangerous.

Mike guided Jake to one of the control panels, showing him how to read the pressure levels and monitor the stabilizer system. The numbers on the screen flickered, the readings shifting every few seconds as the Aqua-Flyer struggled to maintain balance.

"Keep an eye on these two gauges," Mike instructed. "If the pressure starts to spike, let me know immediately."

Jake nodded, his eyes glued to the gauges. He could feel the tension in the air, the weight of responsibility pressing down on him. The numbers flickered again, and Jake's stomach dropped as he noticed the pressure level creeping upward.

"Mike," Jake said, his voice tight with urgency, "the pressure is rising."

Mike's hands moved faster over the controls. "I see it. We're going to need to ascend a bit, but I need to fix this stabilizer issue first. Hang on."

Jake's pulse raced as the Aqua-Flyer shuddered again, the groaning of the hull growing louder. The craft tilted slightly to one side, and Jake could feel the drag of the water pulling them off course. The once-smooth journey had turned into a fight against the forces of nature, and they were losing.

Suddenly, a loud beeping sound filled the cockpit, and red lights flashed across the control panel. Jake's heart leaped into his throat as he glanced at the gauges. The pressure level had spiked dramatically, and the stabilizer system was failing.

"Mike!" Jake shouted, pointing to the flashing red lights. "The stabilizer's out!"

Mike cursed under his breath, his fingers flying over the controls. "We're going to have to ascend—now."

Without another word, Mike adjusted the thrusters, pulling the Aqua-Flyer upward in a rapid ascent. The craft groaned in protest, the pressure outside pushing against the hull with increasing intensity. Jake gripped the armrests, his knuckles white, as the Aqua-Flyer surged upward, the water rushing past them like a dark tunnel.

The beeping continued, louder and more urgent, as the stabilizer system failed completely. The Aqua-Flyer tilted again, and Jake felt the weight of the water pulling them downward, as if the ocean itself didn't want to let them go.

"Come on, come on," Mike muttered, his jaw clenched as he fought to keep the Aqua-Flyer steady.

The cockpit was filled with the sounds of alarms and the groaning of the hull. Jake's heart pounded in his chest, his mind racing with thoughts of what might happen if they couldn't regain control. The pressure was rising, the water pressing in on them from all sides.

"Jake," Mike said, his voice tight but controlled, "I need you to reset the pressure valve system. It's the only way we're going to relieve some of this strain."

Jake's hands trembled as he moved to the controls Mike had pointed out earlier. He had seen Mike operate the pressure system before, but now, with the alarms blaring and the craft shuddering beneath him, the task seemed infinitely more daunting.

"You can do this," Mike said, his voice cutting through the noise. "Just like I showed you. You've got this, Jake."

Taking a deep breath, Jake focused on the control panel. His hands moved quickly, flipping switches and adjusting the pressure valves just as Mike had instructed. The numbers on the screen flickered, and for a moment, nothing seemed to change. But then, slowly, the pressure gauge began to drop, and the beeping subsided.

"You did it!" Mike shouted, a grin spreading across his face. "Nice work, Jake!"

Jake let out a breath he didn't realize he'd been holding, his heart still racing but a sense of relief washing over him. The Aqua-Flyer leveled out, the shuddering easing as the pressure dropped. They were still ascending, but the craft was steady now, the danger passing with each meter they gained.

"That was intense," Jake said, his voice shaky but filled with relief.

Mike nodded, his grin fading into a more serious expression. "It's not over yet. We've stabilized for now, but we need to get back to the surface and check the systems. The stabilizer is still down, and we can't risk another malfunction."

Jake's hands were still trembling, but he felt a surge of pride as he realized what he had just done. He had helped save the Aqua-Flyer, using the skills Mike had taught him. It wasn't just about flying or exploring the ocean—it was about being part of the team, stepping up when it mattered most.

They continued their ascent, the water around them growing lighter as they approached the surface. The tension in the cockpit eased slightly, but Jake could still feel the weight of the situation hanging over them. They weren't out of danger yet, but they were getting closer.

As the Aqua-Flyer broke through the surface of the water, the sunlight streamed in through the windows, casting the cockpit in a warm, golden glow. The ocean stretched out around them, vast and peaceful, a stark contrast to the chaos they had just left behind.

"We made it," Mike said, letting out a breath of relief. "Nice work, Jake. You handled that like a pro."

Jake grinned, his heart still pounding in his chest. "Thanks, Mike. I couldn't have done it without you."

Mike smiled, clapping Jake on the shoulder. "You did great. This was a tough one, but we got through it. And you played a big part in that."

Jake felt a swell of pride in his chest. He had always dreamed of being a pilot, of flying through the skies and exploring new worlds. But today, he had learned something even more important—that being a part of a crew, working together to solve problems and overcome challenges, was just as important as the thrill of adventure.

As they docked the Aqua-Flyer at the research ship, the team of engineers and scientists rushed to meet them, already preparing to inspect the craft for damage. Jake followed Mike out of the cockpit, his legs shaky but his mind still buzzing with the adrenaline of the past hour.

The lead engineer, a man named Dr. Harris, approached them with a clipboard in hand. "We were monitoring the situation from up here," he said, his tone serious. "That was a close call. How's the stabilizer?"

"It's shot," Mike replied, shaking his head. "We'll need to replace it before we can head back down. The pressure was too much, and we lost control for a bit. But Jake here helped reset the pressure system and got us back on track."

Dr. Harris raised an eyebrow, glancing at Jake with an impressed look. "Is that so? Nice work, kid. Not many people would have kept their cool in a situation like that."

Jake felt his face flush with pride. "Thanks. I just did what Mike told me to do."

"You did more than that," Mike said, his tone warm. "You stepped up when it counted. That's what makes a great pilot—and a great team member."

The rest of the team set to work inspecting the Aqua-Flyer, but Jake stayed by Mike's side, his mind still racing with everything that had just happened. He had faced danger before, but this was different. The deep sea was unpredictable, and the challenges it presented were unlike anything Jake had ever encountered.

As the sun began to set on the horizon, casting the sky in hues of orange and pink, Jake sat on the deck of the research ship, staring out at the ocean. The events of the day played over in his mind, and for the first time, he truly understood the risks of exploration. It wasn't just about discovering new places or seeing incredible things. It was about facing the unknown, dealing with the unexpected, and working together to overcome whatever challenges came their way.

Mike joined him on the deck, leaning against the railing as he gazed out at the water. "You okay, Jake?" he asked, his voice gentle.

Jake nodded, though his mind was still processing everything. "Yeah, I'm okay. It was just...a lot."

Mike smiled, his eyes soft with understanding. "It was. But you handled it well. This is what real exploration is like, Jake. It's not always easy, and it's not always safe. But that's what makes it worth it."

Jake thought about that for a moment, letting the words sink in. He had always dreamed of adventure, of flying through the skies and discovering new worlds. But today, he had learned that adventure wasn't just about the excitement—it was about facing the unknown, and finding a way to keep going, even when things got tough.

"I get it now," Jake said quietly. "It's not just about flying. It's about the challenges that come with it."

Mike nodded. "Exactly. And you've shown today that you've got what it takes to handle those challenges."

Jake felt a surge of pride. He wasn't just a kid with a dream anymore. He was part of something bigger, part of a team that was pushing the boundaries of what was possible. And no matter what challenges lay ahead, he knew he was ready for them.

As the stars began to appear in the sky, Jake and Mike stood together, watching the ocean. The deep sea was vast and full of mystery, and Jake knew there was so much left to discover. But now, he wasn't just dreaming about it. He was living it.

Chapter 7: Flight to Safety

The repairs on the Aqua-Flyer were finally complete. After hours of hard work from the engineering team, the stabilizer had been replaced, the systems recalibrated, and the pressure levels and engines carefully checked. The team was confident the craft was ready for its next journey, but there was still an undercurrent of nervous energy among the crew. The malfunction had been a reminder of just how dangerous the deep ocean could be.

Jake stood near the Aqua-Flyer, watching as the final checks were run. His mind was still buzzing from the events of the previous mission. He had faced his fears, stepped up when it mattered most, and helped the team in a critical moment. It was an experience he would never forget. But now, as they prepared to dive back into the depths and eventually transition from water to air, Jake's excitement was tinged with a newfound respect for the dangers they faced.

Mike approached, his expression serious but calm. "We're ready to go, Jake. Everything's checked out. You feeling up for the next leg of the journey?"

Jake nodded, though his heart pounded in his chest. "Yeah, I'm ready."

"Good," Mike said, placing a reassuring hand on Jake's shoulder. "Today's mission is going to be a little different. We're heading back underwater, but this time, we'll be transitioning to flight mid-mission. It's a delicate process, and there's a lot that can go wrong, but I know you've got what it takes to handle it."

Jake swallowed hard, the weight of Mike's words settling over him. Transitioning from water to air was no simple task. The Aqua-Flyer had been designed to handle both environments, but making the shift between them required precision, skill, and focus. One wrong move, and the entire mission could be in jeopardy.

As they boarded the Aqua-Flyer, Jake took his seat beside Mike in the cockpit, the familiar hum of the engines filling the air. The craft had been restored to its full glory, and everything looked pristine, as if the earlier malfunction had never happened. But Jake could still feel the tension lingering in the air. This mission wasn't just about exploration— it was about survival.

The Aqua-Flyer lifted off smoothly from the surface of the water, hovering just above the waves. The sun was beginning to dip below the horizon, casting a golden glow over the ocean. Jake watched as the light danced across the water, creating ripples of color that shimmered in the fading light. It was a beautiful, peaceful moment, but Jake knew it wouldn't last long.

"We'll be diving in just a minute," Mike said, his voice steady as he adjusted the controls. "Once we're back underwater, we'll head to our designated transition point. From there, we'll make the shift to flight.

It's going to be a little tricky, but I've done it before, and I'll guide you through it."

Jake nodded, his hands gripping the armrests as the Aqua-Flyer began to descend. The water rushed up to meet them, and within seconds, they were submerged once again. The light from the surface faded, replaced by the familiar dark blue of the deep ocean. Schools of fish darted by, and the gentle hum of the Aqua-Flyer's thrusters filled the cockpit.

The descent was smooth, and Jake could feel the pressure increasing as they went deeper. But this time, there was no malfunction, no shuddering of the hull. The Aqua-Flyer glided effortlessly through the water, its systems working perfectly. Jake allowed himself to relax, letting the beauty of the underwater world wash over him.

As they descended further, the light from the surface faded completely, and they entered the twilight zone of the ocean. The water here was darker, colder, and the creatures they passed were more alien in appearance. Strange jellyfish floated by, their bodies glowing faintly in the darkness, and Jake spotted a large squid in the distance, its long tentacles trailing behind it like ribbons.

"We're nearing the transition point," Mike said, his voice cutting through the quiet. "This is where things get a little more complicated."

Jake sat up straighter, his nerves buzzing with anticipation. This was it— the moment they had been preparing for. The transition from underwater travel to flight was about to begin.

Mike glanced over at Jake. "Alright, here's the deal. The Aqua-Flyer needs to build enough speed underwater before we can break the surface and take off into the air. It's like launching a plane from a runway, except our runway is the ocean. We'll be using the thrusters to build up speed, and once we're moving fast enough, we'll engage the wings and break through the surface."

Jake nodded, his mind racing with the complexity of the maneuver. Building speed underwater, transitioning to flight—it sounded impossible, but he trusted Mike and the Aqua-Flyer. They had trained for this, designed the craft to handle these exact conditions. But knowing that didn't make it any less daunting.

"The key," Mike continued, "is making sure we hit the right angle when we break the surface. Too steep, and we'll stall out. Too shallow, and we won't get enough lift. We need to time it perfectly."

Jake's hands were sweating as he watched Mike adjust the controls. The Aqua-Flyer began to pick up speed, the thrusters kicking in as they shot forward through the water. The craft's movements became smoother, more fluid, as they accelerated, cutting through the water like a missile.

The pressure inside the cockpit increased as they gained speed, and Jake could feel the weight of the ocean pressing in on them. The water roared around the hull, and the Aqua-Flyer vibrated slightly as the thrusters pushed them forward.

"We're approaching the transition point," Mike said, his eyes focused on the instruments. "Hang on tight, Jake. This is where it gets tricky."

Jake gripped the armrests, his heart pounding in his chest. The Aqua-Flyer was moving faster now, the water rushing past them in a blur. The pressure was intense, but the craft held steady, its design built to withstand the strain.

Suddenly, Mike pulled back on the controls, and the Aqua-Flyer angled upward, heading toward the surface. Jake's stomach lurched as they shot toward the light, the water becoming brighter and clearer with each passing second.

"Here we go!" Mike shouted over the roar of the thrusters.

The Aqua-Flyer surged upward, the surface of the water rushing toward them. Jake braced himself, his heart hammering in his chest. The transition was coming—he could feel it.

And then, in an instant, they broke through the surface.

The transition was like nothing Jake had ever experienced. One moment, they were surrounded by water, the weight of the ocean pressing in on them. The next, they were in the air, the Aqua-Flyer's wings unfurling with a sharp, mechanical hiss. The craft shot upward, water spraying off the hull as they ascended into the sky.

Jake gasped, his eyes wide with awe as the Aqua-Flyer soared into the air. The ocean fell away beneath them, the dark blue waters sparkling in the sunlight. The wings caught the wind, and the craft leveled out, gliding smoothly through the sky.

"We did it!" Jake shouted, unable to contain his excitement.

Mike grinned, his hands steady on the controls. "Nice job, Jake. That was perfect."

The Aqua-Flyer continued to climb, the thrusters shifting to flight mode as they gained altitude. The water on the windows evaporated quickly in the warm air, leaving the cockpit clear. The sky stretched out in front of them, vast and open, a brilliant blue that seemed to go on forever.

Jake couldn't stop smiling. The transition from underwater to flight had been flawless, and now they were soaring through the sky, free from the weight of the ocean. It was like flying in a dream, the Aqua-Flyer responding to every movement with grace and precision.

As they leveled off at cruising altitude, Mike turned to Jake with a proud smile. "You handled that like a pro, Jake. I knew you had it in you."

Jake grinned, his heart still racing with excitement. "That was amazing! I didn't know it could feel like that."

"It's one of the best parts of this job," Mike said, leaning back in his seat. "The transition between water and air—it's like nothing else. You get to experience the best of both worlds."

Jake nodded, his eyes scanning the horizon. The ocean stretched out below them, a shimmering expanse of blue that seemed to go on forever. The clouds floated lazily in the sky, and the sun cast a warm glow over everything. It was peaceful, serene, and Jake felt a deep sense of satisfaction wash over him.

But the moment of peace didn't last long.

Suddenly, the Aqua-Flyer jolted, a sharp, unexpected movement that sent a ripple of panic through Jake. The craft shuddered, and the control panel lit up with flashing red lights. The familiar sound of alarms filled the cockpit, and Jake's stomach dropped.

"What's happening?" Jake asked, his voice tight with fear.

Mike's expression had shifted from relaxed to focused in an instant. His hands flew over the controls, adjusting the thrusters and wings. "We've got turbulence," he said, his voice calm but serious. "A storm system is moving in fast. We need to get above it before it gets any worse."

Jake's heart raced as he glanced out the window. The sky, once clear and peaceful, was now darkening. Thick clouds were forming on the horizon, and Jake could see flashes of lightning in the distance.

"We need to gain altitude," Mike said, adjusting the controls. "Hang on tight, Jake. This could get rough."

The Aqua-Flyer jolted again as they hit another pocket of turbulence. The craft shook violently, and Jake gripped the armrests, his knuckles white. The storm was moving in fast, and the once-serene sky was now filled with swirling clouds and gusts of wind.

Mike pulled back on the controls, and the Aqua-Flyer began to climb. The engines roared as they fought against the turbulence, the craft shaking with every movement. The wind howled outside, and Jake could feel the pressure building inside the cockpit.

"We're going to have to punch through the storm," Mike said, his voice tense. "It's too wide to go around, and we don't have time to wait it out."

Jake's stomach churned at the thought of flying through the storm. The clouds outside were dark and ominous, swirling like a living thing. Lightning flashed in the distance, and Jake could feel the static in the air.

The Aqua-Flyer surged upward, climbing higher into the sky. The turbulence grew worse, the craft shaking violently as the wind battered against the wings. The alarms continued to blare, the red lights flashing across the control panel.

"We're almost there," Mike said through gritted teeth. "Just a little more."

Jake's heart pounded in his chest as the Aqua-Flyer plunged into the storm. The sky outside was dark, filled with swirling clouds and flashes of lightning. The wind howled, and the craft rocked from side to side, fighting to stay on course.

Mike's hands were steady on the controls, his eyes focused on the instruments. He adjusted the wings, compensating for the wind, and the Aqua-Flyer leveled out slightly, though the turbulence was still intense.

"We're going to make it," Mike said, his voice filled with determination. "Just a little further, Jake. We're almost through."

Jake nodded, though his heart was still racing. The storm outside was unlike anything he had ever seen. The clouds swirled around them, and the lightning lit up the sky in blinding flashes. But through it all, the Aqua-Flyer held steady, its powerful engines pushing them forward.

And then, just as suddenly as it had begun, the storm was behind them.

The clouds parted, and the sky opened up in front of them, clear and blue once again. The turbulence faded, and the Aqua-Flyer leveled out, gliding smoothly through the air.

Jake let out a breath he hadn't realized he'd been holding, his body relaxing as the danger passed. The storm was behind them now, a distant memory, and the sky ahead was calm and peaceful.

"We made it," Mike said, a grin spreading across his face. "Nice job, Jake."

Jake smiled, his heart still pounding in his chest. "Thanks, Mike. That was intense."

Mike nodded, his expression proud. "You handled it well. Flying through a storm like that isn't easy, but you stayed calm. That's what matters."

As the Aqua-Flyer continued its journey through the sky, Jake felt a deep sense of accomplishment. He had faced danger, navigated through a storm, and experienced the incredible transition from underwater to flight. It had been a day filled with challenges, but Jake had proven to himself that he could handle whatever the mission threw at him.

The sky stretched out before them, vast and open, filled with endless possibilities. And Jake knew that this was only the beginning of his adventure.

Chapter 8: Mastering the Skies

The Aqua-Flyer soared high above the ocean, its wings cutting through the crisp, clear air with the precision of a finely tuned instrument. After the storm, the skies were calm again, stretching out in every direction with billowy clouds. The tension of their underwater adventure had faded, replaced with the thrilling sensation of pure flight. For the first time, Jake felt what it was like to truly master the skies.

Sitting in the cockpit, Jake couldn't help but marvel at how effortlessly the Aqua-Flyer shifted from its underwater form into a fully-fledged aircraft. The transition had been smooth, and now, with the storm behind them, they were gliding through the sky with a grace that felt almost unreal.

Mike glanced over at Jake, a knowing smile on his face. "I can see it in your eyes, Jake. You're wondering if this thing can fly like a real aircraft, aren't you?"

Jake blinked, a little surprised at how easily Mike had read his thoughts. "Well... yeah. I mean, I know it's an amphibious craft and all, but can it really handle like an actual plane?"

Mike chuckled, leaning back in his seat. "I had the same doubts when I first flew this thing. But trust me, the Aqua-Flyer is more than just a hybrid. Once we get up here, she flies just like any top-tier aircraft. Maybe even better."

Jake felt a thrill shoot through him. "Better?"

Mike's grin widened. "Oh, yeah. We've got the best of both worlds—speed, agility, and stability. You want to see what she can really do?"

Jake's heart leaped in his chest. "Absolutely."

"Alright then," Mike said, cracking his knuckles as he reached for the controls. "Buckle up, because we're about to take this bird through its paces."

Jake quickly tightened his seatbelt, his pulse racing with excitement. He had experienced the Aqua-Flyer in the water and seen its underwater capabilities, but now, he was about to witness what it could do in the air. And if Mike's confidence was any indication, it was going to be something spectacular.

Mike took the controls, his hands steady and precise. "First, let's start with some basic maneuvers. Steep turns."

He adjusted the yoke, and the Aqua-Flyer banked sharply to the right, its wings tilting at a steep angle as they entered the turn. Jake felt the pull of G-forces pressing him back into his seat as the aircraft looped gracefully through the air. The horizon tilted sharply, and for a moment, it felt like they were almost vertical.

"This is a steep turn," Mike explained, his voice calm despite the sharp angle. "It's a basic maneuver, but it's a great way to test an aircraft's handling. Notice how smooth the turn is? No shaking, no instability. The Aqua-Flyer holds steady, even at these extreme angles."

Jake's eyes widened as he looked out the window. The world spun beneath them, the ocean a blur of blue and white, but the Aqua-Flyer felt rock solid, as if it were on rails. There was no wobbling, no sign of strain—just pure, fluid motion.

"That's incredible," Jake said, his voice filled with awe. "It's so smooth."

"Yup," Mike said, easing the plane out of the turn. "Now, let's try something a little more advanced. Ever heard of a Dutch roll?"

Jake frowned, trying to recall the term from one of the many books he'd read about aviation. "Isn't that when the plane rolls from side to side, like a weaving motion?"

"Exactly," Mike said, clearly pleased with Jake's knowledge. "It's a maneuver that tests an aircraft's lateral stability. It's tricky to pull off, but the Aqua-Flyer can handle it like a pro. Watch this."

Mike adjusted the ailerons and rudder, and suddenly the Aqua-Flyer began to roll gently from side to side, its wings tilting back and forth in a smooth, rhythmic motion. The nose of the aircraft stayed level, but the plane itself rocked from left to right, like a boat swaying in the water.

Jake felt his stomach flip as the plane rolled, but the motion was surprisingly controlled, almost graceful. He could feel the balance of the aircraft, how each roll was perfectly countered by the opposing motion, keeping them steady even as they tilted from side to side.

"This is the Dutch roll," Mike said, his voice calm. "It's a test of lateral control. If the aircraft has any instability, you'd feel it here. But the Aqua-Flyer? She's built for this. Notice how balanced the roll is? No oscillation, no over-correction. Just smooth, controlled motion."

Jake nodded, gripping the armrests as they continued to roll. "It feels...balanced. Like it's meant to do this."

Mike smiled, easing the plane out of the Dutch roll. "That's the beauty of this design. We've got the aerodynamic profile of a fighter jet, but with the stability of a commercial plane. Now, how about something a little more thrilling?"

Jake's heart raced. "More thrilling than that?"

"Oh, yeah," Mike said, his grin widening. "Let's try a barrel roll."

Jake's eyes widened. A barrel roll? That was a maneuver he had only ever seen in movies and video games. It involved rolling the plane in a complete circle, looping it through the air like a rollercoaster. The thought of experiencing one in real life made Jake's pulse quicken with both excitement and nerves.

Mike adjusted the throttle, and the Aqua-Flyer picked up speed, the engines humming with power. Then, with a swift movement, he pulled back on the yoke and twisted the ailerons. The nose of the Aqua-Flyer tilted upward, and before Jake knew it, they were spinning through the air.

The world outside spun in a blur of blue sky and white clouds as they rolled through the air. Jake's stomach dropped, and he let out an involuntary gasp as they flipped upside down for a brief moment. But despite the dizzying motion, the Aqua-Flyer remained stable, its movements controlled and precise.

"Whoa!" Jake shouted, unable to contain his excitement.

Mike laughed, clearly enjoying himself. "That's a barrel roll, kid! Feels pretty wild, doesn't it?"

Jake nodded, his heart still racing. "That was amazing! I can't believe it handled that so well!"

Mike grinned, pulling the Aqua-Flyer out of the roll and leveling off. "Told you this thing flies like a real aircraft. She's got agility, speed, and control. But we're not done yet."

Jake's pulse quickened again. "What else can it do?"

Mike's expression grew more serious, though the excitement in his eyes was still clear. "How do you feel about a spin?"

Jake blinked. "A spin? Like... a stall?"

"Exactly," Mike said, nodding. "We're going to intentionally put the Aqua-Flyer into a stall and enter a spin. It's a risky maneuver, but it's a great way to test an aircraft's recovery capabilities. Most planes can get into trouble if they don't recover from a spin properly, but the Aqua-Flyer is designed to handle it. You up for it?"

Jake swallowed hard. He had read about stalls and spins before, and he knew they could be dangerous if not handled correctly. But Mike was a seasoned pilot, and if he said the Aqua-Flyer could handle it, Jake trusted him.

"I'm ready," Jake said, though his voice was a little shaky.

"Good," Mike said, his expression focused. "Just hang on, and don't panic. I've got this."

With that, Mike eased back on the throttle, slowing the Aqua-Flyer's speed. The nose of the plane tilted upward as they lost speed, and Jake could feel the aircraft beginning to struggle against the lack of lift. The airspeed dropped, the engines hummed quieter, and then suddenly, the Aqua-Flyer stalled.

For a brief moment, everything felt weightless. The nose of the aircraft dropped sharply, and Jake felt his stomach lurch as the plane tilted downward. The world outside spun violently as the Aqua-Flyer entered a spiral dive, the horizon twisting and turning in a dizzying blur.

Jake gripped the armrests tightly, his heart pounding in his chest. The feeling of falling was intense, but Mike's calm demeanor reassured him.

"We're in a spin now," Mike said, his voice steady. "This is where most pilots lose control. But the Aqua-Flyer? Watch this."

With precise movements, Mike adjusted the rudder and ailerons, countering the spin. The plane responded instantly, leveling out of the dive and pulling up smoothly. Within seconds, they were flying straight and level again, the spin completely neutralized.

Jake let out a breath he hadn't realized he'd been holding. "That was... that was insane."

Mike chuckled, clearly pleased. "Yeah, it's a bit of a rush, isn't it? But as you can see, the Aqua-Flyer handles it like a champ. We've got built-in recovery systems that help us pull out of spins, but it's still up to the pilot to handle it correctly."

Jake nodded, his heart still racing with the thrill of the spin. He had read about these kinds of maneuvers in books, but experiencing them firsthand was a whole different story. The Aqua-Flyer wasn't just a hybrid craft—it was a true aircraft, capable of handling some of the most advanced and complex maneuvers with ease.

"You want to try something?" Mike asked, glancing over at Jake.

Jake blinked, his excitement returning. "You mean... fly it?"

"Yeah," Mike said with a grin. "I think you're ready. I'll walk you through some basic maneuvers, and then you can try a few advanced ones. What do you say?"

Jake's pulse quickened. This was what he had dreamed of his whole life—flying an aircraft, feeling the control in his hands, and performing real aviation maneuvers. He swallowed his nerves and nodded.

"I'm ready."

Mike smiled, his confidence in Jake clear. "Alright. Let's start with some simple turns. Take the yoke, and I'll guide you through it."

Jake reached for the controls, his hands trembling slightly with a mixture of excitement and anxiety. He felt the weight of the yoke beneath his fingers, the power of the Aqua-Flyer humming through the cockpit. This was it—the moment he had been dreaming of for as long as he could remember.

"Start with a shallow turn to the left," Mike instructed. "Nice and easy."

Jake nodded, easing the yoke to the left. The Aqua-Flyer responded immediately, banking smoothly as they entered the turn. Jake felt the G-forces press against him, but the motion was fluid, controlled. He grinned, the thrill of flying filling him with pure joy.

"That's it," Mike said, his voice filled with pride. "Now, try a steeper turn."

Jake adjusted the yoke, increasing the angle of the turn. The Aqua-Flyer banked sharply, the horizon tilting as they looped through the air. The sensation of control, of guiding the aircraft through the skies, was exhilarating.

"Perfect," Mike said. "Now let's try a roll."

Jake's heart raced as he adjusted the ailerons, initiating the roll. The Aqua-Flyer flipped through the air, the world spinning around them as they completed the maneuver. Jake's stomach flipped, but the sensation was thrilling, not frightening. He had done it—he had flown the Aqua-Flyer through a roll.

"That was incredible!" Jake shouted, his voice filled with excitement.

Mike laughed. "You're a natural, Jake. Keep it up. You want to try a barrel roll?"

Jake's eyes widened. "You think I can handle it?"

Mike grinned. "I know you can."

With Mike's guidance, Jake initiated the barrel roll. The Aqua-Flyer tilted upward, and then they were spinning through the air, the world a blur of sky and clouds. Jake felt the thrill of the motion, the exhilaration of controlling such a powerful machine. It was everything he had dreamed of and more.

As they leveled out, Jake's heart pounded with excitement. He had flown the Aqua-Flyer, performed real aerial maneuvers, and experienced the true power of flight. The sky stretched out before them, vast and endless, filled with possibilities.

"You did great, Jake," Mike said, his voice filled with pride. "You've got the makings of a real pilot."

Jake grinned, his heart swelling with pride. "Thanks, Mike. That was... that was everything I've ever dreamed of."

Mike smiled, his eyes soft with understanding. "And this is just the beginning. There's so much more to explore, so much more to learn. But you've proven that you've got what it takes. The sky's the limit now, Jake."

As the Aqua-Flyer glided through the air, Jake felt a deep sense of satisfaction wash over him. He had faced his fears, mastered the skies, and proven to himself that he was capable of flying like a real pilot. The adventure wasn't over—it was just beginning.

The sun dipped low on the horizon, casting a warm, golden light over the ocean below. The world stretched out before them, vast and beautiful, filled with endless possibilities. And Jake knew, deep in his heart, that he was ready for whatever came next.

Chapter 9: Returning to the Surface

The Aqua-Flyer glided through the golden skies, the setting sun casting long shadows over the vast expanse of the ocean below. After a day filled with excitement, tense moments, and extraordinary maneuvers, Jake found himself staring out at the endless horizon, his heart filled with a mixture of pride, awe, and exhaustion. He had flown. Not just piloted a simulation or read about it in books, but truly flown through the air, performed aerial stunts, and experienced the raw power of an aircraft. The weight of that realization was still settling in.

As the sky began to shift from golden hues to a soft purple twilight, Mike adjusted the controls, bringing the Aqua-Flyer into a steady glide. The high-energy excitement of the earlier flight had given way to a peaceful calm. The Aqua-Flyer, now fully transitioned into its role as an aircraft, moved through the air like it belonged there, perfectly in tune with the wind currents and the wide-open sky.

Mike glanced over at Jake, who was still staring out of the window, lost in thought. "You've had quite a day, huh?" Mike said, his voice breaking the silence but with a softness that matched the tranquil atmosphere around them.

Jake turned to Mike, a grin spreading across his face. "I still can't believe it. I mean... I flew a plane! And not just any plane, but this one— an amphibious craft that can fly and dive! It's like something out of a dream."

Mike chuckled. "I had that same feeling the first time I took this beauty out. It's hard to believe a machine can handle both the sky and the deep sea. But she's built for it. And so are you, Jake."

Jake's heart swelled with pride at Mike's words. This wasn't just a casual compliment; it was validation from someone he respected deeply, someone who knew what it took to be a pilot, to navigate through uncharted territory both above and below the surface.

"I never imagined it would feel like this," Jake admitted, his voice quieter now, reflective. "I always thought flying would be the most amazing thing in the world, but after everything we've been through today... it's even better than I imagined. And the ocean... there's so much I didn't know."

Mike nodded, his eyes scanning the horizon. "The ocean and the sky— they're not so different, you know. Both are vast, full of mysteries, and require a steady hand to navigate. The same principles that apply to flight apply to exploring the deep. It's all about balance, control, and staying calm when things get rough."

Jake thought back to their near-emergency underwater, the pressure malfunction, and how Mike had stayed so calm and focused, guiding them through the crisis. It was in those moments that Jake had learned the most—not just about flying, but about what it meant to be part of a team, to face danger and still keep going.

As they flew in silence for a few more minutes, Jake's thoughts drifted back over the entire mission. From the moment they had taken off for the first time, to the breathtaking descent into the ocean depths, to the heart-pounding moments of turbulence and mechanical failure. Every challenge had tested him, and each time, he had learned something new about himself, about the Aqua-Flyer, and about the incredible possibilities that lay ahead.

The sun had dipped low, casting a soft glow over the horizon, when Mike's voice broke the peaceful silence again. "We're getting close to base. Time to start thinking about our descent."

Jake snapped out of his thoughts, his attention shifting back to the task at hand. The journey wasn't over yet. They still had to bring the Aqua-Flyer down safely, transitioning from air to sea-level landing.

"Are we landing on water again?" Jake asked, remembering the earlier transition from underwater to air.

Mike nodded. "Yep, but this time, we're going the other way. We'll be descending gradually, and once we get low enough, we'll switch to water mode and land smoothly on the ocean's surface."

Jake couldn't help but feel a surge of excitement. He had experienced the thrilling transition from sea to sky, but this—this was a chance to see how the Aqua-Flyer handled landing back on water, the opposite direction. Another opportunity to witness its dual capabilities.

Mike began the descent, and the Aqua-Flyer responded with the same grace and precision that had impressed Jake earlier. They dropped altitude slowly, the horizon rising as the ocean grew closer. Jake's stomach fluttered slightly as the plane tilted downward, and he gripped the armrests with a mixture of excitement and anticipation.

The water below gleamed under the fading sunlight, the waves calm and serene. Jake watched as they approached the surface, the ocean growing larger and larger with each passing second. Mike's hands were steady on the controls, adjusting the flaps and thrusters to prepare for the transition.

"Okay, here we go," Mike said, his voice steady and calm. "I'm switching us into water-landing mode. Keep your eyes on the horizon and stay calm. The key is to make contact with the water at the right angle."

Jake nodded, his heart racing as the Aqua-Flyer descended closer to the water. He could hear the soft hum of the engines, the rush of wind as they cut through the air. The ocean loomed ahead, vast and endless, like a mirror reflecting the sky.

The Aqua-Flyer dropped lower, and lower, until finally, with a soft hiss, the plane's hull touched the surface of the water. Jake braced himself for impact, but it wasn't needed. The transition was smooth, almost seamless. The Aqua-Flyer glided across the water's surface, its powerful engines slowing their thrust as the craft settled into a gentle float.

"We're down," Mike said, letting out a breath. "Smooth as silk."

Jake couldn't stop the grin that spread across his face. "That was incredible. It felt like we barely even touched the water."

Mike chuckled, clearly pleased with the landing. "That's what you want in a water landing. Smooth, controlled, and no sudden jolts. You handled the transition perfectly."

Jake felt a wave of pride wash over him. He had been part of the entire process, from flight to landing, and now, with the Aqua-Flyer floating gently on the ocean's surface, he felt like he had completed a full-circle journey.

Just as Jake was settling into the calm, something caught his attention. A faint, low sound—almost like a rumble—vibrated through the hull. Jake frowned, glancing over at Mike.

"Do you hear that?" Jake asked, his voice tinged with concern.

Mike's expression shifted instantly from relaxed to focused. He adjusted the controls, his eyes narrowing as he listened. The low rumble grew louder, more distinct, and Jake could feel a slight vibration in the seat beneath him.

"What is that?" Jake asked, his heart beginning to race again.

Mike's hands flew over the controls, checking the instruments and diagnostics. "Something's not right. The engine isn't responding like it should. I'm getting some abnormal readings from the right thruster."

Jake's stomach tightened. After everything they had been through, was another emergency unfolding now?

"Is it serious?" Jake asked, trying to keep his voice steady.

Mike's jaw tightened as he continued to run through the diagnostics. "Could be. It might just be a minor issue with the thruster, but I'm not taking any chances. We're close to base, so I'm going to bring us in as quickly and safely as possible."

Jake nodded, his heart pounding as the Aqua-Flyer began to pick up speed again, this time skimming across the water as Mike aimed for their base on the horizon. The rumbling sound continued, growing louder with each passing moment, and Jake could feel the vibrations intensifying beneath him.

"We've got a potential engine failure," Mike said, his voice calm but firm. "Stay focused, Jake. We've been through worse."

Jake nodded, trying to keep his nerves in check. The base was in sight now, a small dot on the horizon growing larger as they approached. But the rumble beneath the Aqua-Flyer was getting worse, the vibrations shaking the entire craft now.

Mike adjusted the controls, trying to stabilize the Aqua-Flyer as it skimmed across the surface of the water. The right thruster sputtered, and Jake could feel the craft veering slightly to the right, fighting to stay on course.

"Come on, hold steady," Mike muttered under his breath, his hands moving quickly over the controls.

The base was getting closer, but so was the threat of an engine failure. Jake gripped the armrests, his eyes fixed on the approaching dock. They were almost there. Just a few more minutes.

Suddenly, the right thruster cut out completely, and the Aqua-Flyer lurched to the side, veering off course. Jake's stomach dropped as the craft tilted sharply, the left engine straining to keep them afloat.

"Mike!" Jake shouted, panic rising in his throat.

"I've got it!" Mike said, his voice sharp with focus. He adjusted the controls, compensating for the loss of the right thruster. The Aqua-Flyer wobbled, but Mike's steady hands kept it from tipping over.

The base was just ahead, and Mike pushed the remaining engine to its limits, guiding the Aqua-Flyer toward the dock. The craft shuddered and groaned, the single engine roaring as it fought to keep them on course.

"Almost there," Mike said, his jaw clenched with concentration.

The dock loomed ahead, and with one final push, the Aqua-Flyer slid into position, the remaining engine sputtering as it came to a stop. The craft bobbed gently on the water, the vibrations finally subsiding as the engine cut out completely.

Jake let out a breath he hadn't realized he'd been holding, his heart racing from the tension of the last few minutes. They had made it. Just barely, but they had made it.

Mike sat back in his seat, his hands trembling slightly from the adrenaline. "That was close," he said, his voice quiet but steady. "Too close."

Jake nodded, still catching his breath. "What happened?"

Mike ran a hand through his hair, shaking his head. "Looks like the right thruster gave out. Could be a mechanical failure, or it could be the pressure from the earlier dive. Either way, we're lucky it didn't happen while we were still in the air."

Jake's heart pounded in his chest, but he managed a shaky smile. "Yeah... that would have been bad."

Mike turned to Jake, his expression softening. "You did great out there, Jake. You kept your cool, even when things got tough. That's what makes a great pilot."

Jake smiled, though his legs still felt shaky from the near-emergency. "Thanks, Mike. I just... I didn't want to mess up."

"You didn't," Mike said firmly. "You did exactly what you needed to do. And because of that, we're safe."

As the team of engineers rushed to inspect the Aqua-Flyer, Jake and Mike climbed out of the cockpit, their feet hitting the solid dock. The sun had finally set, and the stars were beginning to appear in the night sky, twinkling above the calm ocean.

Jake stood there for a moment, staring up at the stars, his mind racing with everything that had happened. The flight, the underwater exploration, the tense moments of danger, and finally, the safe return. It had been a journey unlike anything he had ever experienced, one that had tested him in ways he hadn't expected.

But now, as he stood on solid ground, surrounded by the sounds of the night and the gentle lapping of the waves, Jake felt a deep sense of accomplishment. He had faced the unknown, navigated through danger, and come out stronger on the other side.

As Mike stood beside him, staring up at the same stars, Jake knew that this was just the beginning. The sky and the ocean held endless possibilities, and Jake was ready for whatever came his way.

Chapter 10: The Minds Behind the Machine

The next morning, the base hummed with quiet efficiency. The previous day's mission had been a success, but now the real work of fine-tuning and improving the Aqua-Flyer had begun. Jake watched from a distance as engineers and technicians swarmed around the craft, their movements purposeful, their focus intense. He had always admired pilots and explorers, but now he was starting to realize that the people behind the scenes—the ones who built and maintained the aircraft—were just as important.

Jake found himself wanting to learn more about them. After all, the Aqua-Flyer wasn't just a marvel of nature—it was a feat of human ingenuity. Without the expertise and hard work of the engineers and scientists, none of this would have been possible. And the more Jake thought about it, the more he realized that he knew very little about what went into creating something as complex and innovative as an amphibious aircraft.

As if sensing Jake's curiosity, Mike appeared beside him, a cup of coffee in hand. "You look like you've got something on your mind," he said with a knowing smile.

Jake shrugged, his gaze still on the Aqua-Flyer. "I was just thinking about how amazing it is that people actually built this thing. I mean, I understand flying it, but I don't really know how it works—how it was designed or how they made it all come together."

Mike grinned. "You've got the right idea. Flying is only part of the story. The real magic happens before you even get in the cockpit—when the engineers and scientists are figuring out how to make something like the Aqua-Flyer a reality."

Jake's interest piqued even more. "Do you think I could meet them? The people who built it, I mean."

Mike chuckled. "I was hoping you'd ask that. Follow me. I'll introduce you to the team."

Jake's heart raced with excitement as he followed Mike across the base, past the technicians still working on the Aqua-Flyer. They entered a large building that housed the engineering labs and workshops. Inside, the atmosphere was buzzing with activity. Tables were piled high with tools, schematics, and models of various aircraft components. Computers lined the walls, displaying complex designs and simulations. It was a world Jake had never seen up close, but one that immediately fascinated him.

Mike led Jake through the labyrinth of workstations and introduced him to the people who had made the Aqua-Flyer a reality. The first person they met was Dr. Olivia Garcia, the lead aeronautical engineer. She was in her late thirties, with long light brown hair and a no-nonsense expression, but her eyes lit up as she talked about her work.

"Jake, meet Olivia," Mike said. "She's the brains behind the Aqua-Flyer's aerodynamic design."

Olivia smiled and offered Jake a firm handshake. "Nice to meet you, Jake. I hear you've been helping Mike with some of the test flights."

Jake nodded, feeling a bit in awe. "Yeah, but I don't know much about how the Aqua-Flyer was actually designed. How did you even come up with something that can fly and dive into the ocean?"

Olivia laughed, clearly used to such questions. "It took a lot of years and a lot of trial and error. The idea was to create something that could operate efficiently in two completely different environments—air and water. That meant designing wings and control surfaces that could retract or adjust depending on the medium. Aerodynamics and hydrodynamics are two very different beasts, but we've managed to make them work together."

She motioned to a large computer monitor displaying a 3D model of the Aqua-Flyer. "Here, check this out."

Jake leaned in as Olivia pulled up a simulation of the Aqua-Flyer transitioning from air to water. She explained how the wings folded back during the dive to reduce drag and how the thrusters rotated to provide propulsion once the craft was submerged. She showed him the complex system of valves and pressure seals that kept the aircraft watertight even at extreme depths.

"It's all about balance," Olivia said. "In the air, you want minimal drag and maximum lift. In the water, you need to minimize resistance and focus on stability. Every design decision was a trade-off between those two environments, and it took years to get it just right."

Jake was amazed. "I can't believe how much goes into this. It's like designing two different vehicles and then combining them into one."

Olivia nodded. "Exactly. And the fun part is, we're always learning and improving. Every mission gives us new data, new challenges to solve. It's never boring, I can tell you that."

They spent a few more minutes discussing the finer details of the Aqua-Flyer's design before Mike led Jake to another section of the lab, where they met Ben, the chief propulsion engineer. Ben was tall and lanky, with grease-stained hands and a mischievous grin that suggested he loved tinkering with engines more than anything else.

"Jake, this is Ben," Mike said. "He's the one who makes sure the Aqua-Flyer actually moves."

Ben wiped his hands on a rag and gave Jake a nod. "Hey, kid. I hear you got to experience our little engine issue yesterday."

Jake nodded. "Yeah, the right thruster gave out. I thought we were in real trouble."

Ben laughed. "Yeah, I heard about that. The Aqua-Flyer's a great machine, but like anything else, she's not perfect. That's why we're constantly tweaking and testing."

Jake watched as Ben worked on a model of the Aqua-Flyer's thruster system, explaining how the dual-propulsion system allowed for efficient movement both in the air and underwater. He showed Jake the hybrid engine design, which could switch between jet propulsion in the air and water propulsion when submerged.

"Most aircraft engines are designed to work in just one environment," Ben explained. "But the Aqua-Flyer needs to function in two completely different mediums. That means we had to develop a propulsion system that could handle both. The thrusters are equipped with variable pitch blades, which allows us to adjust the thrust depending on whether we're in air or water. It's like having two engines in one."

Jake stared in fascination as Ben pulled apart a model of the engine, revealing the intricate workings inside. "So how do you keep the engines from flooding when you dive into the water?"

"Good question," Ben said, clearly impressed by Jake's curiosity. "We've got a series of valves that close off the air intakes and reroute the propulsion system to use the water around us. It's all about managing pressure and keeping the water where it's supposed to be—outside the engine."

Jake couldn't help but be amazed by how much thought and precision went into every detail of the Aqua-Flyer's design. From the aerodynamics to the propulsion system, every component had to work perfectly in sync for the craft to perform as it did. It was a testament to the incredible minds behind the machine.

As they moved to the next section of the lab, Jake met Sarah, the systems integration specialist. She was responsible for making sure all the different parts of the Aqua-Flyer worked together seamlessly. With a background in software engineering and robotics, Sarah had designed the control systems that allowed the pilot to transition between air and water modes with the flick of a switch.

"Think of the Aqua-Flyer as a big puzzle," Sarah explained as she showed Jake a diagram of the aircraft's control systems. "Each piece— whether it's the engine, the wings, or the underwater thrusters—has to communicate with the others. My job is to make sure everything works together as a cohesive system. If one part fails, the whole thing could be in jeopardy."

Jake watched as Sarah pulled up a simulation showing how the control systems adapted during different phases of flight. She explained how the computer onboard the Aqua-Flyer constantly monitored conditions, adjusting the aircraft's settings to optimize performance in both air and water.

"Without the integration of these systems, the pilot would have to manually adjust every little thing," Sarah said. "But with the right software, the Aqua-Flyer can make those adjustments in real-time, allowing the pilot to focus on the mission."

Jake was impressed by the complexity of it all. It wasn't just about designing a cool vehicle—it was about making sure every part of it worked in harmony, from the wings to the engines to the onboard computers. It was a level of teamwork and coordination that he had never fully appreciated before.

As the day went on, Jake continued to meet more members of the team—materials specialists who had developed the lightweight, high-strength composite materials that made the Aqua-Flyer both fast and durable, robotics experts who had designed the mechanical arms for underwater exploration, and marine biologists who worked with the engineers to ensure the craft could safely explore fragile underwater ecosystems.

By the time the tour was over, Jake's head was spinning with all the new information. He had always admired the pilots and explorers, but now he realized that the real heroes behind the Aqua-Flyer were the people who had worked tirelessly behind the scenes to make it a reality.

As they walked back toward the Aqua-Flyer, Mike turned to Jake with a smile. "So, what do you think?"

Jake grinned, though his mind was still racing. "I think it's amazing. I never realized how much goes into something like this. It's not just about flying—it's about designing, building, and making sure everything works together."

Mike nodded. "That's right. Being a pilot is great, but there's a whole world of possibilities out there beyond the cockpit. The people you met today—they're the ones who make it all possible. Without them, we wouldn't be able to explore the skies or the ocean."

Jake looked around the base, watching the engineers and technicians still hard at work. For the first time, he felt like he truly understood the scope of what went into building something like the Aqua-Flyer. It wasn't just about technology—it was about teamwork, creativity, and pushing the boundaries of what was possible.

"Do you think I could do something like that one day?" Jake asked, his voice filled with excitement.

Mike smiled. "I think you can do anything you set your mind to, Jake. Whether you want to be a pilot, an engineer, a scientist, or something else entirely—it's all about following your passion and working hard to make it happen."

Jake nodded, feeling more inspired than ever. The Aqua-Flyer had opened his eyes to a world of possibilities, and now, he knew that his dreams weren't limited to just flying. There was a whole universe of discovery and innovation out there, and Jake was ready to explore it all.

Chapter 11: The Forces of Flight and Submersion Explained

The Aqua-Flyer rested peacefully in its dock, the sunlight glinting off its sleek metallic surface. After the high-paced adventure of the last few missions, Jake found himself back on solid ground, standing at the edge of the platform and gazing at the marvel that had taken him both through the skies and beneath the ocean's depths. But today, he wasn't thinking about where the Aqua-Flyer could take him. He was thinking about how it worked, how this incredible machine could soar through the air and dive into the ocean with such ease.

In the cockpit, flying felt natural, as though the Aqua-Flyer was simply an extension of the pilot. But Jake knew it was far more complicated than that. Every movement, every dive, every turn was governed by forces Jake didn't fully understand. He had heard the engineers talk about aerodynamics, buoyancy, and hydroplanes, but the details were fuzzy in his mind.

Determined to learn more, Jake made his way to the research facility, where Olivia, the lead aeronautical engineer, spent most of her time when she wasn't overseeing the Aqua-Flyer's operations. He had questions, and he knew Olivia was the perfect person to answer them. Her knowledge of the craft seemed limitless, and she had a way of explaining even the most complex concepts in a way that made sense to someone like Jake, who was just starting to explore the technical side of things.

As Jake entered the lab, he was greeted by the sight of engineers working on various components of the Aqua-Flyer. They were surrounded by monitors displaying data from recent missions, 3D models of the aircraft, and the occasional burst of animated conversation as they discussed the latest adjustments. It was a hive of activity, a place where science and engineering merged to create something truly extraordinary.

Olivia spotted Jake from across the room and waved him over. She had been reviewing some of the flight data from their last mission, but she could tell from the look on Jake's face that he was here for something different.

"Curiosity got the better of you again, huh?" Olivia said with a smile as Jake approached her station.

Jake grinned, nodding. "Yeah, I've been thinking a lot about how the Aqua-Flyer works. I mean, I get the basics, but I want to understand more—especially about the forces that act on the aircraft when we're flying and when we're underwater."

Olivia's eyes lit up. This was one of her favorite topics. "You've come to the right place. The forces that govern flight and submersion are fascinating, and understanding them is key to appreciating just how remarkable the Aqua-Flyer really is. Have a seat, and let's dive in."

Jake pulled up a chair beside Olivia as she brought up a detailed 3D model of the Aqua-Flyer on her screen. The model rotated slowly, showing the aircraft from every angle. Jake marveled at the sleek lines, the expertly crafted wings, and the complex system of thrusters and control surfaces that allowed the craft to operate in two very different environments.

"Let's start with flight," Olivia said, tapping a few keys to highlight the wings of the Aqua-Flyer. "When we're flying, there are four main forces at play: lift, weight, thrust, and drag. These forces are always interacting with each other, and understanding them is the **foundation of aerodynamics**."

Jake nodded, eager to learn. He had heard these terms before, but he wanted to know how they actually worked together. "I know lift keeps us up and thrust pushes us forward, but how do they balance out?"

Olivia smiled, pleased that Jake was already thinking about balance. "Exactly. It's all about balance. Let's break them down one by one, starting with lift. Lift is the force that opposes gravity and keeps the aircraft in the air. It's generated by the shape of the wings."

She pointed to the curved shape of the Aqua-Flyer's wings on the screen. "These wings are designed with a specific curvature that allows air to flow faster over the top surface than it does underneath. That difference in speed creates a pressure difference, with lower pressure on top and higher pressure below. This pressure difference generates lift, which pushes the aircraft upward."

Jake stared at the model, imagining how the air would flow over the wings as the Aqua-Flyer soared through the sky. "So the faster we go, the more lift we generate?"

"Exactly," Olivia confirmed. "The faster the air moves over the wings, the greater the lift. But it's not just lift we have to think about. There's also weight—essentially the force of gravity pulling us down. Weight is always trying to bring the aircraft back to the ground, so the amount of lift we generate has to be strong enough to counteract that."

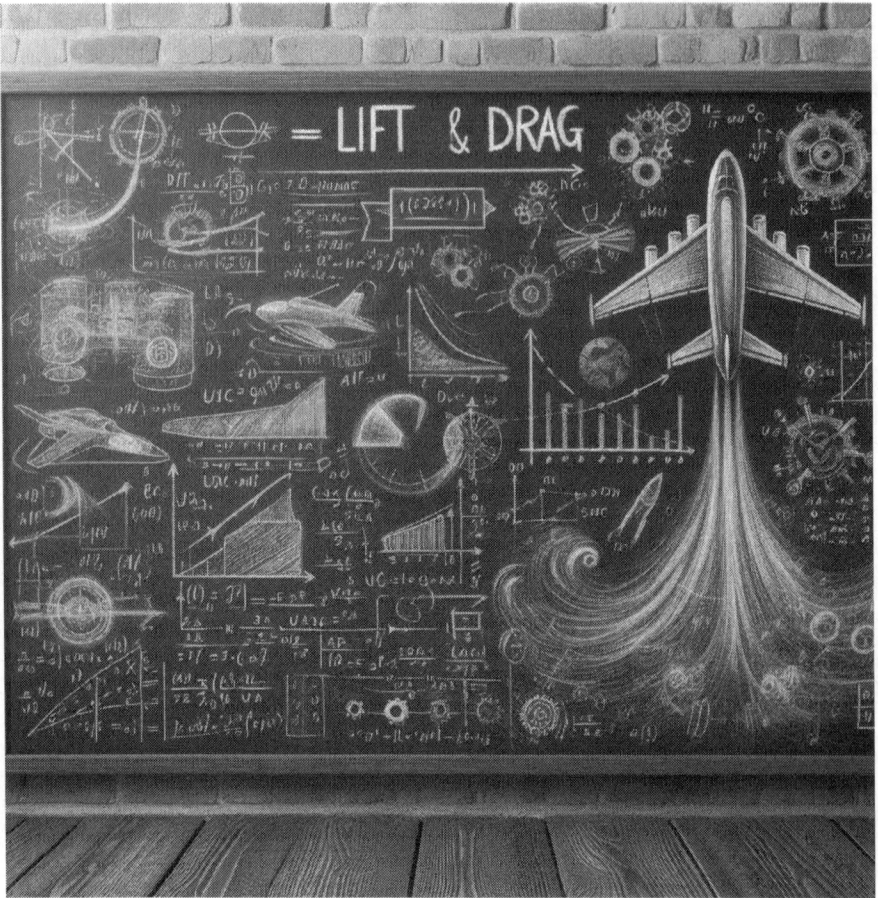

Jake thought about the balance between those two forces—lift pushing the aircraft up and weight pulling it down. It was like a constant tug-of-war. "And thrust is what gives us the speed we need to generate that lift, right?"

"Right again," Olivia said, nodding. "Thrust comes from the engines. It's the force that propels the aircraft forward through the air. Without thrust, we wouldn't be able to move fast enough to generate the lift we need to stay airborne."

She tapped a key, and the model shifted to highlight the Aqua-Flyer's powerful jet engines. "These engines provide the thrust that pushes us forward. They're designed to be efficient both in the air and underwater, which is one of the things that makes the Aqua-Flyer so unique. But in the air, it's all about providing enough thrust to overcome drag."

Jake tilted his head, trying to remember what he knew about drag. "Drag is like air resistance, right? It's what slows us down?"

Olivia smiled. "Exactly. Drag is the force that opposes our motion. As the aircraft moves through the air, it has to push against the air molecules in its path. The faster we go, the more drag we encounter. That's why the Aqua-Flyer is designed to be as aerodynamic as possible. We want to minimize drag and maximize thrust."

Jake thought about the sleek, streamlined design of the Aqua-Flyer. Its smooth curves and sharp angles seemed perfect for cutting through the air with minimal resistance. It made sense now why aerodynamics was so important—without it, the aircraft would waste too much energy fighting against drag.

"So, when we're flying, it's all about balancing those four forces—lift, weight, thrust, and drag," Jake said, summarizing what he had learned so far. "Lift pushes us up, weight pulls us down, thrust moves us forward, and drag slows us down."

Olivia beamed, clearly impressed by how quickly Jake was picking up the concepts. "Exactly. And that's what makes flying such an incredible balancing act. Every time we change speed, altitude, or direction, those forces shift. It's up to the pilot and the aircraft's design to keep everything in balance."

Jake leaned back in his chair, trying to wrap his mind around all the different forces at play during flight. It was amazing to think that every time they took off, they were managing a complex interplay of forces that kept the Aqua-Flyer stable in the air.

"But that's just flight," Olivia said, her voice taking on a new level of excitement. "When we go underwater, things get a lot more interesting."

Jake's curiosity spiked. He had experienced the thrill of diving into the ocean with the Aqua-Flyer, but he hadn't given much thought to the science behind it. "What happens when we're underwater? How do the forces change?"

Olivia pulled up a new diagram on her screen, this time showing the Aqua-Flyer submerged beneath the ocean's surface. "Underwater, we're no longer dealing with the same forces as we are in the air. In the air, it's all about aerodynamics. But underwater, it's about **hydrodynamics**. The main forces we need to think about are buoyancy, water resistance, and gravity."

Jake leaned forward, fascinated by the shift in focus. "Buoyancy—that's what makes things float, right?"

"Exactly," Olivia said, nodding. "Buoyancy is the force that pushes objects upward when they're submerged in a fluid, like water. It's caused by the pressure of the water surrounding the object. The deeper you go, the higher the pressure. If the force of buoyancy is greater than the object's weight, it will float to the surface. If it's less, the object will sink."

She pointed to the Aqua-Flyer's hull, which was designed to be both airtight and watertight. "To control our buoyancy, we use ballast tanks. By adjusting the amount of water in these tanks, we can control whether the Aqua-Flyer floats, sinks, or hovers at a specific depth."

Jake remembered hearing about ballast tanks in submarines. It made sense now that the Aqua-Flyer would use a similar system to navigate underwater. "So, when we're underwater, it's like balancing buoyancy and gravity the same way we balance lift and weight in the air."

Olivia smiled. "Exactly. Buoyancy wants to push us up, and gravity wants to pull us down. If we're too buoyant, we'll float uncontrollably to the surface. If we're too heavy, we'll sink to the bottom. So, we adjust the ballast tanks to keep the Aqua-Flyer at the right depth."

Jake imagined the delicate balance between those two forces, much like the balance between lift and weight in the air. It was all about control, making sure the forces worked together to keep the craft stable.

"But there's more to moving underwater than just buoyancy," Olivia continued. "We also have to deal with water resistance, which is like drag in the air. Water is about 800 times denser than air, so moving through it requires a lot more energy."

She pointed to the thrusters on the Aqua-Flyer's model. "These thrusters provide the propulsion we need to move through the water. They work like the engines in the air, but they're designed to push water instead of air. And since water is so much denser, the thrusters have to work a lot harder."

Jake thought about how the Aqua-Flyer had felt underwater, the slow, steady movement as they glided through the ocean. It made sense that the craft had to work harder to move through the water compared to the air. "So, it's kind of like moving through syrup—everything slows you down?"

Olivia laughed. "That's one way to put it. Water resistance is much stronger than air resistance, so we need more power to move efficiently. And that's where our hydroplanes come in."

Jake had heard the word before but didn't fully understand what hydroplanes did. "Hydroplanes are like underwater wings, right?"

"Exactly," Olivia said, bringing up an image of the Aqua-Flyer's hydroplanes. "Just like the wings in the air generate lift, hydroplanes help us control our movement underwater. By adjusting the angle of the hydroplanes, we can control our depth and direction. If we angle them upward, we can rise toward the surface. If we angle them downward, we can dive deeper."

Jake watched as Olivia demonstrated how the hydroplanes worked, tilting them up and down to show how they affected the Aqua-Flyer's movement. It was fascinating to see how similar the principles of flight and underwater navigation were, even though the forces at play were different.

"So, the hydroplanes are like the control surfaces on a plane, but for underwater movement," Jake said, piecing it together.

"Exactly," Olivia said. "They give us precise control over our depth and direction, allowing us to move smoothly through the water. Without them, we'd be at the mercy of buoyancy and water resistance. The hydroplanes, along with the thrusters, give us the maneuverability we need to navigate underwater."

Jake was amazed by how much thought and precision had gone into every aspect of the Aqua-Flyer's design. It wasn't just about making it fly or making it dive—it was about making sure it could transition smoothly between two very different environments while managing the unique forces of each.

"As you can see," Olivia said, "the Aqua-Flyer is a perfect example of how we can combine the principles of aerodynamics and hydrodynamics. In the air, we focus on lift, weight, thrust, and drag. Underwater, we deal with buoyancy, gravity, water resistance, and the use of hydroplanes. It's a delicate balance, but when everything works together, it allows the Aqua-Flyer to operate in both environments seamlessly."

Jake leaned back in his chair, still processing everything he had learned. It was incredible to think that every time they flew or dived, they were managing a complex interplay of forces that kept the Aqua-Flyer stable and efficient. It wasn't just about technology—it was about physics, engineering, and a deep understanding of how the world worked.

He realized that what made the Aqua-Flyer so remarkable wasn't just its ability to fly or dive. It was the way it handled the challenges of both environments, using the forces of flight and submersion to its advantage. Every detail, from the shape of the wings to the design of the thrusters to the placement of the hydroplanes, had been carefully crafted to make the impossible possible.

Jake left the research facility that day with a new sense of awe for the Aqua-Flyer and the team of engineers who had brought it to life. He had always loved the thrill of flying, but now he understood that there was so much more to it than just getting in the cockpit and taking off. The forces of flight and submersion, the balance between lift and weight, buoyancy and gravity—it was all part of a delicate dance that made the Aqua-Flyer the extraordinary machine it was.

As he walked back to the dock, where the Aqua-Flyer waited for its next mission, Jake couldn't help but smile. He had learned so much about the science behind the craft, and yet there was still so much more to discover. The forces of nature were complex, but with the right knowledge and ingenuity, they could be harnessed to achieve incredible things.

Chapter 12: The Future of Amphibious Flight

As the sun rose higher in the sky, casting a warm glow over the ocean and the bustling base, Jake found himself in the heart of the action. The engineers, scientists, and technicians he had met over the past few days were working together, fine-tuning the Aqua-Flyer, gathering data from the recent missions, and discussing how they could push the technology even further.

Today felt different. There was a sense of purpose and excitement in the air—like they were on the cusp of something big, something that would change the world. The Aqua-Flyer was no longer just an experimental craft; it was a glimpse into the future, a tool that could revolutionize the way humans explored the world, both above and below the surface.

Jake stood with Mike on a high observation deck that overlooked the base and the wide expanse of the ocean beyond. From here, he could see the Aqua-Flyer gleaming in the sunlight, its sleek body a testament to human ingenuity. In just a few short days, Jake had learned more than he ever thought possible—about aviation, engineering, marine biology, and, most importantly, about himself.

"Hard to believe this is only the beginning," Mike said, leaning against the railing and looking out at the ocean. His voice was filled with a mix of pride and anticipation. "The Aqua-Flyer has already proven it can handle some of the toughest conditions on Earth. But there's so much more we can do with it. So much more we need to explore."

Jake nodded, his thoughts swirling with everything he had experienced. "I never realized how much potential this thing has. It's not just about flying or diving—it's about discovering new worlds."

Mike glanced at Jake, a small smile playing at the corners of his mouth. "Exactly. The Aqua-Flyer isn't just an aircraft or a submersible—it's a bridge between two worlds. And right now, we're only scratching the surface of what it can do."

As they stood there, Mike began explaining the broader vision for the Aqua-Flyer. The aircraft had started as an ambitious project to combine flight and underwater exploration, but as the team had developed it, they realized its potential extended far beyond that. The Aqua-Flyer wasn't just a machine; it was a gateway to the future of amphibious flight, a future where air and sea were no longer separate domains but interconnected spaces for exploration.

"We're looking at a future where the Aqua-Flyer could be used in all kinds of applications," Mike said, his gaze still fixed on the horizon. "From scientific research to military operations, from environmental conservation to search and rescue. The possibilities are endless."

Jake listened intently, his mind racing with the implications. He had already seen how the Aqua-Flyer could revolutionize marine research, giving scientists access to parts of the ocean that were previously unreachable. But now, Mike was talking about something even bigger— about how amphibious flight could change the way humans interacted with the planet, and perhaps even with space.

"You mentioned military applications before," Jake said, curious to learn more. "How exactly would the Aqua-Flyer be used in that way?"

Mike nodded. "There are a lot of potential uses. For one, the Aqua-Flyer's ability to transition from air to water makes it perfect for search and rescue missions, especially in remote or dangerous areas. Imagine a scenario where a ship is stranded at sea or a plane crashes in the ocean. Traditional aircraft might struggle to land or rescue people in time, but the Aqua-Flyer could dive straight in, locate survivors, and bring them to safety."

Jake pictured the scene in his mind—an emergency at sea, with the Aqua-Flyer swooping in to save the day. It made sense. The craft's versatility made it ideal for rapid-response missions, where every second counted.

"And it's not just search and rescue," Mike continued. "The military is also interested in using the Aqua-Flyer for underwater surveillance and reconnaissance. Submarines are great for stealth operations, but they're slow and can't easily transition to the surface. The Aqua-Flyer can operate like a submarine, but when it needs to move quickly, it can break the surface and take off into the air. That kind of flexibility is a game-changer."

Jake's eyes widened. He hadn't thought about the military applications in such depth before, but now it was clear just how valuable the Aqua-Flyer could be in strategic situations. Being able to move between air and water, adapt to changing environments, and gather intelligence in ways that no other craft could—this was the future of military operations, and the Aqua-Flyer was at the forefront of that revolution.

"What about environmental research?" Jake asked, his thoughts shifting back to the more peaceful applications of the technology. "How could the Aqua-Flyer help with that?"

Mike smiled, clearly pleased with Jake's curiosity. "Environmental research is one of the most important areas where the Aqua-Flyer can make a difference. With climate change and environmental degradation threatening marine ecosystems, we need better tools to monitor and protect the ocean. The Aqua-Flyer can dive deep into fragile ecosystems, like coral reefs and hydrothermal vents, without causing damage. It allows scientists to gather data, observe marine life, and study the impact of human activity in real time."

Jake thought back to the hydrothermal vents they had explored during the mission. The strange, otherworldly creatures they had encountered were part of an ecosystem that had remained largely untouched by human hands—until now. But with the Aqua-Flyer, scientists could study these environments without disturbing them, ensuring that the delicate balance of life in the deep sea remained intact.

"And it's not just about studying the ocean," Mike added. "The Aqua-Flyer can also help with conservation efforts. For example, it could be used to track endangered species, monitor illegal fishing activity, or even help clean up oil spills. Its ability to transition from air to water means it can cover large areas quickly, and that makes it an invaluable tool for protecting the planet."

Jake was amazed by the range of possibilities. The Aqua-Flyer wasn't just a cool machine—it was a tool that could make a real difference in the world. Whether it was helping scientists uncover the mysteries of the deep sea, aiding in search and rescue missions, or protecting fragile ecosystems, the Aqua-Flyer was paving the way for a new era of exploration and conservation.

As they continued to talk, Mike revealed that there were even discussions about using the Aqua-Flyer for space exploration. Jake's eyes widened at the thought.

"Space?" Jake asked, his voice filled with wonder. "How could the Aqua-Flyer help with that?"

Mike smiled, clearly excited by the idea. "Think about it. Some of the moons in our solar system—like Europa and Enceladus—are covered in ice, but scientists believe there could be oceans beneath the surface. If we can develop a craft that can transition between air and water here on Earth, why not adapt that technology to explore other worlds? The Aqua-Flyer, or a version of it, could one day be used to explore alien oceans, searching for signs of life beneath the icy crust of distant planets."

Jake's mind raced with the possibilities. The idea of taking the Aqua-Flyer to other planets, to explore oceans that had never been touched by human hands, was beyond anything he had ever imagined. It wasn't just about exploring Earth anymore—it was about exploring the universe.

As the conversation shifted back to Earth, Jake and Mike discussed the next steps for the Aqua-Flyer. The team was already working on new versions of the craft, incorporating the data and lessons learned from the recent missions. There were plans to build larger, more advanced models that could travel farther, dive deeper, and fly higher than ever before.

"The sky's the limit," Mike said with a grin. "Or maybe the ocean's the limit. Either way, we're just getting started."

Jake couldn't help but feel a surge of excitement. The future of amphibious flight was wide open, and he was lucky enough to be a part of it. But more than that, he had learned that the real innovation wasn't just in the technology—it was in the people who worked together to make it happen. From the engineers to the scientists to the pilots, it was a team effort, and every person played a crucial role in pushing the boundaries of what was possible.

As the day drew to a close, Jake and Mike headed back toward the base, where the rest of the team was gathered for a final debriefing. Jake had never felt more inspired. The future was full of possibilities, and with the Aqua-Flyer leading the way, there was no telling what they might discover next.

Before they entered the base, Jake paused, looking back at the Aqua-Flyer one last time. He thought about everything he had learned—the technology, the teamwork, the challenges and rewards of exploration. He realized that this wasn't just the end of a mission—it was the beginning of a new chapter in human exploration.

"The future is bright, Jake," Mike said, noticing the look on his face. "And you're a part of it now."

Jake smiled, feeling the weight of those words. The future of amphibious flight was just beginning, and he was ready to dive headfirst into whatever came next.

--The End

Conclusion: Lessons Learned

As Jake reflected on his journey with the Aqua-Flyer, he realized that the incredible experience he had been part of was built on far more than just exciting flights and underwater dives. Beneath the surface of each mission was a foundation of ingenuity, focus, education, and above all, commitment. Creating something as revolutionary as the Aqua-Flyer required more than just passion—it demanded vision, resources, and an unwavering dedication to seeing the project through. These were the true lessons Jake had learned, not just about the Aqua-Flyer itself, but about what it took to push the boundaries of what was possible.

One of the first things Jake had come to understand was the power of **focus**. From the very beginning, every member of the team had been laser-focused on their goal: to create a craft that could seamlessly transition between air and water, exploring both environments with equal efficiency. This wasn't a project that could be completed with half-hearted effort. It required complete dedication, not just for days or months, but for years.

Jake had seen that kind of focus in the engineers he met—people like Olivia, Ben, and Sarah—who spent countless hours refining the design, testing new ideas, and solving problems that had no easy answers. It wasn't enough to just have an idea; they had to be relentless in their pursuit of perfection. When the Aqua-Flyer faced challenges, whether mechanical or environmental, the team didn't give up. They went back to the drawing board, revised their approach, and kept pushing forward. It was a lesson in persistence that Jake knew would stay with him for the rest of his life.

Focus wasn't just about solving technical problems. It was about knowing what the end goal was and staying on course, even when obstacles arose. The Aqua-Flyer team had a clear vision of what they wanted to achieve, and that vision guided every decision they made. Whether it was testing the aerodynamics in flight or ensuring the thrusters worked underwater, they never lost sight of their mission. That level of focus was critical, and Jake realized that it applied not only to large-scale projects like the Aqua-Flyer but to personal goals as well. Without focus, dreams remained just that—dreams.

Then there was **ingenuity,** the lifeblood of the Aqua-Flyer project. Every aspect of the craft, from its design to its propulsion system to its software, was a result of human ingenuity—of people thinking outside the box and finding creative solutions to complex problems. Jake had been awed by the innovation he saw, particularly in the way the team combined technologies that didn't typically work together.

Aerodynamics and hydrodynamics were completely different fields of study, yet the engineers had found a way to merge them seamlessly. They had created wings that folded underwater, engines that transitioned from air to water propulsion, and systems that could adapt in real-time to changing conditions. This was no small feat. It took years of trial and error, constant revision, and a willingness to try new ideas, even when the risks were high.

Jake realized that ingenuity wasn't just about having a good idea—it was about execution. It was about taking those ideas and finding ways to make them work in the real world. The Aqua-Flyer's success didn't come from a single breakthrough moment. It came from hundreds of small innovations, each building on the last, until the team had created something that was truly groundbreaking. This process of continuous improvement, of taking risks and learning from failures, was something Jake knew he could apply to his own life, no matter what path he chose.

But ingenuity alone wasn't enough. Without the right **education** and knowledge, the Aqua-Flyer project would have never gotten off the ground. The engineers, scientists, and technicians Jake had met were all experts in their fields. They had spent years—sometimes decades—studying aerodynamics, propulsion, software engineering, marine biology, and more. Their education was the foundation upon which the Aqua-Flyer was built.

Jake had always loved learning, but this experience showed him just how important education was to achieving great things. It wasn't just about getting good grades or passing tests—it was about developing the skills and knowledge needed to solve real-world problems. The team behind the Aqua-Flyer had mastered their respective disciplines, and that mastery allowed them to innovate in ways that would have been impossible otherwise.

Jake also saw that education was an ongoing process. Even the experts he had met were constantly learning, adapting to new challenges, and staying on the cutting edge of technology. Whether it was learning new programming languages to refine the Aqua-Flyer's control systems or studying the latest developments in material science to improve the craft's durability, the team was always evolving. This commitment to lifelong learning was something Jake admired deeply and knew he would need to embrace in his own future.

As he thought about education, Jake also realized that none of this would have been possible without **development money** and **investment**. Building the Aqua-Flyer required more than just brilliant ideas and technical know-how—it required significant financial resources. The research and development process was expensive, from the initial design phase to the testing of prototypes to the final construction of the aircraft. Every stage of the project required funding, and without that investment, the Aqua-Flyer would have remained a concept on paper.

Jake had never really considered how much money went into projects like this before. He had always assumed that once you had a good idea, the rest would fall into place. But now he understood that innovation came with a price tag. From the state-of-the-art materials used to build the Aqua-Flyer to the advanced simulations and testing facilities required to ensure its safety, everything cost money.

It wasn't just about securing a one-time grant or investment. The project required **sustained financial support** over the years, with backers who believed in the vision and were willing to commit long-term. Jake realized that in order to make big things happen, you needed people who were willing to take financial risks, who believed that the investment would pay off in the form of new technology, new discoveries, and new opportunities.

As Jake reflected on the importance of investment, he also thought about the **huge commitments** that had been made by the team. These weren't people who clocked in and out like it was just another job. They had committed years of their lives to this project, working long hours, sacrificing personal time, and dedicating themselves fully to the vision of the Aqua-Flyer. It wasn't easy work. There were countless setbacks, moments of frustration, and times when success seemed far away. But they never gave up.

Jake realized that commitment was what separated good ideas from great accomplishments. Anyone could have a good idea, but it took commitment—long-term dedication and perseverance—to turn that idea into reality. The Aqua-Flyer existed because the people behind it had made the decision to see it through, no matter how difficult the road ahead became. They had invested not only their time and money but their hearts and souls into the project.

That commitment also extended beyond the technical team. Jake knew that Mike, as a pilot, had put in countless hours flying test missions, gathering data, and pushing the Aqua-Flyer to its limits. His role wasn't just about flying—it was about ensuring the craft was safe, efficient, and ready for real-world applications. Mike's commitment to the project was just as important as the engineers' commitment to the design. Everyone had a role to play, and everyone's contribution was essential.

As Jake reflected on these lessons, he realized that the journey of the Aqua-Flyer mirrored his own personal growth. He had arrived at the base as a young boy with dreams of flying, but he was leaving with a new understanding of what it took to make those dreams a reality. It wasn't just about passion—it was about hard work, focus, education, financial investment, and, above all, commitment.

The lessons he had learned weren't just about technology or aviation. They were lessons about life. If he wanted to achieve great things, whether in aviation, engineering, or any other field, he would need to apply those same principles. He would need to stay focused on his goals, embrace ingenuity and creative problem-solving, continue his education, and seek out the resources and investments necessary to make his dreams a reality.

Jake also realized that no one accomplished great things alone. Just as the Aqua-Flyer had been built by a team of dedicated professionals, any future success Jake hoped to achieve would require collaboration and teamwork. He had learned the importance of surrounding himself with people who shared his vision and who brought their own expertise and ideas to the table.

As Jake prepared to leave the base and return home, he knew that this experience would shape the rest of his life. The Aqua-Flyer had opened his eyes to a world of possibilities, and the lessons he had learned would stay with him forever. He wasn't just dreaming of flying anymore—he was dreaming of how he could contribute to the world, how he could take the lessons of focus, ingenuity, education, investment, and commitment, and apply them to whatever challenges lay ahead.

The future was full of possibilities, and Jake felt ready to face them. Whether it was through aviation, engineering, or something else entirely, he knew that the path to success wasn't always easy, but it was always worth it.

Made in the USA
Middletown, DE
09 February 2025